WHAT PEOPLE ARE SAYING ABOUT

PREPARING FOR A WORLD THAT DOESN'T EXIST – YET

Many people recognize the world is changing. From all walks of life and diverse political perspectives, they fear that preparing for the still existing but disappearing world may leave them high and dry. For most people this is a cause of anxiety and frustration. Rick Smyre and Neil Richardson are unusual, if not unique, in envisioning the world that is being born in a way that gives real guidance to those who will live in it. Their contribution is, to put it mildly, extraordinary.

John B. Cobb, Jr., Founding Director of the Center for Process Studies.

This is a fascinating and timely book that is sure to change the way you think about the past, present, and especially the future. Imagine a world that did not exist when the book was written, yet, which was destined to manifest itself at some time in history, and that moment might be just on the horizon. The first moment I set eyes on this manuscript and considered what it means, I got its implications intuitively and my mind was quickly changed by them. Yet I had to put it down for a few days to catch my breath, and think through its implications. "We're living on the precipice of a new era in human history," write the authors. We had better get ready for an emerging society that will be increasingly inter-connected, interdependent, and complex (as the authors rightly say,) or we will be in deep trouble. This means that we need new ideas to help humanity adapt during the emerging "Second Enlightenment" of our global species. In order to prepare for the changes ahead we need effective leadership and Transformational Wisdom, which the book provides. By Second Enlightenment, the authors mean a new democratic vision, a higher view of our current international forms of democracy, whether in Higher Education, Health and Wellness, Governance or the Economy. The book does not just complain about the present crises we are feeling in our democracy, it offers many pragmatic solutions in an age that I have called *Spiritual Democracy*.

"Whereas change historically has come from the top down," says Richardson and Smyre, "we believe that developing new capacities in local communities will transform not only our own daily lives, but the lives of everyone and everything on the planet." This is no light statement; its aim is to get readers to think big, to completely change the way we think, by leading us to our own book of knowledge within. What is needed, therefore, are new types of leaders to take us forward into an age where connective thinking and generative dialogue will lead to synthesis and new ideas. The result will be essentially a more spiritually and environmentally rich democracy.

Steven Herrmann, Ph.D Jungian Psychotherapist, MFT Author of *Spiritual Democracy: The Visions of Early American Visionaries for the Journey Forward*

The First Enlightenment (roughly 1740 – 90) gave the world modernity – notably modern science, modern economics and modern government. For a long time, these brought great benefits to many people, particularly in health, knowledge, and material comfort. However, modernity is now well past its sell-by date. Most, if not all, of the big problems of our time can be traced back, one way or another, to modernity's overwhelming focus on materialism. Happily, a Second Enlightenment is already under way. Although it is not yet possible to describe it fully, it will surely be much kinder to this planet and it will almost certainly value the spiritual as much as the material.

This book by Rick Smyre and Neil Richardson is, in my view, an important contribution to the Second Enlightenment, in at least three respects: it shows that radical change, on the part of all of us, is a necessity, not an optional extra; it puts emphasis on the local, as well as the global; and it provides a very practical guide to leaders, managers and others who want to engage actively in the deep, all pervading changes that are abroad in the world today. For many of us, change does not come easily. We prefer the familiar, the known, even when this no longer works for us! However, and this is the underlying message of this book, all of us will have to venture into unknown territory and try things that may, at first, feel very strange, if we hope to survive and thrive in this rapidly changing world. Scary? Yes, of course, but very exciting and very necessary. Speaking personally, my hope is that the Second Enlightenment will enable us, at last, to be the intelligent species that we are capable of being. We will be an asset to the planet rather than, as at present, a liability. Now, that is really something to look forward to!

Chris Thomson, author of "Full Spectrum Intelligence"

Preparing for a World that Doesn't Exist – Yet:

Creating a Framework for Communities of the Future

Preparing for a World that Doesn't Exist – Yet:

Creating a Framework for Communities of the Future

Rick Smyre & Neil Richardson

IOWA CITY
DISCARDED
from Iowa City Public Library
PUBLIC LIBRARY

CHANGE
MAKERS
BOOKS

Winchester, UK
Washington, USA

First published by Changemakers Books, 2016
Changemakers Books is an imprint of John Hunt Publishing Ltd., Laurel House, Station Approach,
Alresford, Hants, SO24 9JH, UK
office1@jhpbooks.net
www.johnhuntpublishing.com
www.changemakers-books.com

For distributor details and how to order please visit the 'Ordering' section on our website.

Text copyright: Rick Smyre & Neil Richardson 2015

ISBN: 978 1 78535 451 9
Library of Congress Control Number:

All rights reserved. Except for brief quotations in critical articles or reviews, no part of this
book may be reproduced in any manner without prior written permission from the publishers.

The rights of Rick Smyre & Neil Richardson as authors have been asserted in accordance with the
Copyright, Designs and Patents Act 1988.

A CIP catalogue record for this book is available from the British Library.

Design: Stuart Davies

Printed and bound by CPI Group (UK) Ltd, Croydon, CR0 4YY, UK

We operate a distinctive and ethical publishing philosophy in all
areas of our business, from our global network of authors to
production and worldwide distribution.

CONTENTS

In memory of Marietta and Fred, deeply loving parents who gave me courage and hope; and in honor of Brownie, wonderful wife and best friend who feeds my soul, and Cinda, Deric, Beth, Dana, Caleb, Ian, Aidan and Kiefer, children and grandchildren whom I treasure who have given me immense joy. Rick

And

To my parents, Dave and Rudy Richardson who let me become who I am, Richard Hough, Abdul Aziz Said and Richard Harwood for showing me how to use my gifts and to Karen Loeschner and Kai Richardson for showing me who I am. Love always, Neil

Whatever affects one directly, affects all indirectly
Dr. Martin Luther King

Acknowledgement of People Important to the Evolution of COTF from 1989-2016

John Abbot (DC), Jennifer Adams (NE), Steve Ahlenius (TX), Dan Anderson (IA) Simon Anderson (MI), Howard Arbuckle, Margaret Arbuckle (NC), Mack Arrington (NC), Rob Atkinson (DC), Randy Austin (NC), Paul Aydelott (TN), Sandy Babb (NC), Chevon Baccus (FL), David Baldwin (OH), Keith Bandy (NC), Patrick Barlow (WI), Glenn Barth (IL), Gerry Bartels (GA), Timlynn Batitsky (IA), Don Beck (TX), Ted Becker (AL), Rob Bencinni (NC), Beatrice Benne (CA), Howard Benson (GA), Renee Bernier (Canada), Dr. Peter Bishop (TX), Terry Bledsoe (NC), George Boggs (CA), John Bost (NC), Shana Bourcier (PA), Hal Bouton (NC), J.C. Bowman (TN), LaDene Bowen (IA), Julie Broadway (ME), Anita Brown-Graham (NC), Bliss Brown (FL), Ronnie Bryant (NC), Matt Buccelli (DC), Benita Budd (NC), George Bullard (SC), Frank Burns (DC), Paul Candveri (PA), Robin Cape (NC), Tanya Carter (VA), Henry Cauthen (SC), Marvin Cetron (VA), Tim Chase (KS), Jay Chatzel (TX), Michael Childress (KY), Tom Christoffel (VA), Ann Cline (KY), Chuck Coates (KY), Dr. John Cobb (CA), Elyse Cochran (GA), Dr. Andrew Cohill (VA), John Cook (VA), Paul Cook (KY), Wayne Corley (VA), Phil Coyle (NC), Ned Crosby (MN), William Crossman (CA), Ron Crouch (KY), Jim Damicis (ME), Diedre Crow (SC), Brian Crutchfield (NC), Storm Cunningham (DC), Wade Den Hartog (IA), Alex Deleuse (CA), Barry Denk (PA), Maggie de la Teja (TX), Dee Dickinson (WA), Gary Donaldson (VA), Henry Doss (NC), Dr. Ed Duffy (SC), Donald Duncan (NC), Gwen Dungy (DC), Dr. Hank Dunn (WVA), Steve Dunnivant (FL), Doug Eason, (NC), Rick Dubose (KY), Terry Dugan (CA), Don Eberly (PA), Susan Echard (DC), Gary Edmonds (OR), Joel Embry (FL), J ohn Enamait (NC), Kathy Evert (KS), Chuck Ewart (SC), Dave Faulkner (OH), Tom Fauquet (OH), Chris Fenwick

(PA), Ellen Ferber (VA), Darci Fersch (CA), John Findlay (MA), Karl Fisch (CO), Matt Fitzgerald (VA), Bev Fitzpatrick (VA), Dr. Jayne Fleener (NC), Dr. Kathryn Fletcher (NY), Madilyn Fletcher (SC), Jay Forrest (TX), Matt Forshee (GA), Tom Forsythe (TN), July Fort (TX), Bob Fuller (NC), Joy Gaash (MI), Ashok Gangedean (PA), Nicole Garzino (CA), Jay Gary (CO), Chris Gates (CO), Margaret Gayle (NC), Bob Gayle (SC), Karen Geiger (NC), Ernest Gerlach (TX), Scott Gibbs (RI), Virginia Gibbs, (GA), Mark Gignac (VA), Gaila Gilliland (NE), Allen Goben (TX), Jim Godwin (SC), Milton Gold (NC), Jack Gottsman (CA), Fabienne Gaux-Baudiment (France), Stanford Green (CA), Butch Grove (NC), Steve Grove (IL), Sally Goerner (NC), Ron Gonsolley (NE), Tim Grooms (NC), Larry Grossman (CT), Gary Gute (IA), Matthew Haggis (Scotland), Bill Halal (DC), Billy Ray Hall (NC), Mark Hall (NE), Win Hallett (AL), Bill Hammerman (CA), Linda Harrill (NC), Dewey Harris (NC), Cecilia Harry (NE), Rich Harwood (DC), Jack Healy (CT), Danny Hearn (NC), Greg Heineman (NE), Doug Henton (CA), Barbara Herchmer (Canada), Jay Herson (DC), Paul Hewitt (DC), Elina Hiltunen (Finland), Ray Hoag (MI), Hollie Hollister (MN), Lin Hollowell (NC), Steve Holt (AL), Jerry Hopkins (VA), Myles Hopkins (South Africa), Steve House (KY), Jim Houton (KY), Fiona Howard (Scotland), Neil Howe (VA), Lauren Huddleston (CO), Kim Humfrey (KY), Ken Hunter (MD), Victor Hwang (CA), Phil Hyatt (TN), Jan Inglis (Canada), Nat Irvin (KY), Zoltan Istvan (CA), Seth Itzkan (MA), Gus Jacacci (VT), Lewis Jaffe (PA), Art Jackson (NC), Michael Jackson (England), Lewis Jaffe (PA), Manish Jain (India), Michelle James (DC), David Jameson (SC), Curtis Johnson (MN), Joseph Johnson (GA), Steve Johnson (MD), Dr. Ben Judkins (KY), Prasad Kaipa (CA), David Kalinchuk (Canada), Karen Jackson (KY), Dick Kelso (ME), Jim Kerley (FL), Betty Kettman (OK), David Key (GA), Freddie Killough (NC), Joseph Kilpatrick (NC), Don Kirkman (NC), Jack Kiser (NC), Landon Kite (FL), Eric Klein (NV), John Knott (SC), Susan Knox

(GA), George Kripner (NC), Amy Kritzer (NY), Joseph Kruth (NV), Henry Kwok (Singapore), Bruce LaDuke (KY), Bob Lahm (TN), Tom Lamb (PA), Sarah Langer (NC), Colleen LaRose (NJ), Bob LaSala (FL), Mike Latta (NC), Paul Laurienti (NC), Kay LaVerne (NE), Barbara Lawrence (NC), Robert Leaver (CT), Graham Leister (England), Tom Lesnak (MO), Janine LaSueur (NY), Stewart Levine (CA), Michael Lewis (IL), Tom Lombardo (AZ), Jean Craig Long (NC),Nancy Love (NC), Sylvia Lovely (KY), Carolyn Lukensmeyer (AZ), Pam Lung (CA), Alice Lutz (NC), Larry Lytle (NC), Tim Mack (DC), Bob Madsen (VA), Leo McGuire (SC), Steve McCullough (TX), Dr. Frank Maletz (CT), Stan Mandel (NC). Oliver Markley (TX), Bob Martin (FL), D. G. Martin (NC), John Martin (VA), Gary Marx (VA), Matt Pirvanik (OK), Dan Mauk (NE), Sandy Maxey (NC), Catherine McCall (Scotland), Gloria McCall (KY), Kate McAllum (CA), Rick McClurd (NC), Bill McCoy (NC), James Mceachin (NC), Dwight McInvaill (SC), Starin McKeen (CO), Jo McLaughlin (MD), Rick McLean (NC), Sharon McMillian (NC), Ron McQuaid (Scotland), Dr. Michael Manning (NC), Fred Mednick (WA), Devin Meisinger (NE), Betsy Merkel (OH), Gary Merrill (CA), Scott Meruci (OH), Jessica Metta (OR), Maria Meyers (MO), John Migliaccio (NY), John Milewski (VA), Clarence Miller (GA), Ira Miller (NC), Melissa Mills, (NC), George Martin (NC), Rex Miller (TX), Eduardo Millet (TX), Billy Mills (NC), Bill Minnis (TX), Fred Monk (SC), Ians Mooers (KY), Rick Moorefield (WVA), John Moran (CA), Doug Morley (PA), Sharon Morris (CO), Suzanne Morse (VA), Bob Munro (FL), Sue Murdock (NC), Helene Nawrocki (PA), Andy Nelson (OR), Lavon Nelson (IL), Ruben Nelson (Canada), Jared Nichols (NC), Michale Nolan (NE), Moses Nueman (NC), Michelle Nunn (GA), Valerie Oberle (NC), Vicki O'day (MI), Gary O'Grady (MO), Ken Oilschlager (MS), Akinwale Ojomo (DC), Obina Okeke (SC), Gwen Oneal (NC), Fred Opilinski (PA), Hugh Osborn (NY), Per Ostling (Sweden), Gary Ostroske (LA), Jonathon Packer (TX), Randy Patrick

(Canada), Jane Patterson (NC), Susan Patterson (NC), Mickey Paysour (NC), Mack Pearsall (NC), Lucy Penegar (NC), Richard Penegar (NC), Clovis Perry (NC), David Pierce, (IL), Matt Pivarnik (OK), Joy Pooler (PA), John Popoff (Canada), Katherine Prince (OH), Paul Privateer (AZ), Robin Pulver (NC), David Punchard (FL), Patricio Salinas (Chile), Bill Randall (NC), Betty Chapin Rash (NC), Michelle Ratcliff (MO), Sally Rawlins (TX), Linda Ray (NC), Mike Ribble (KS), Kathy Rice (TX), Jonathon Richter (MT), Vern Riediger (Canada), Ed Rikel (KY), Rob Camoin (NY), Cheryl Roberts (NC), Robin Rhyne (NC), Ivon Rohrer (NC), Nancy Roof (DC), Boyd Rose, Kathleen Rose (NC), (GA), Scott Ross (NV), Charlie Rowe (NC), Barry Russell (SC), Steve Rust (AR), Elisabet Sahtouris (HI), R. J. Sandoval (TX), William Sarine (IN), Jessica Saunders (OH), Lisa Sax (NY), Cindy Shilling (VA), Robert Schley (CA), Leslie Scott (NC), Mark Scott (TX), Dr. Steve Scott (NC), Brent Schulthorp (NC), Bill Seabrook (NC), Charlie Shappard (TX), Harold Shapiro (SC), Phil Sharre (TN), Roger Sheats (NC), John Shemo (CT), Ed Shenk (CA), Arthur Shostak (CA), Rupam Shrivastave (NJ), Bill Shuffstall (PA), Alan Silverstein (MD), Mike Simon (AL), Dr. Lauri Sims (NC), John Sink (NC), Mark Skillstead (NC), Skip Skinner (VA), R.B. Sloan (TX), Oksana Slobazhan (Russia), Curtis Smeby (MT), Dr. James Smith (SD), Jerry Smith (AK), John-Paul Smith (NC), Judi Smith (NC), Mary Smith (NC), Mihaela Smith (London, UK), Ron Smrek (OH), Lili Song (China), Frank Sowa (PA), Bill Spencer (NC), Frank Spencer (GA), John Spratt (SC), Rick Starks (KY), Dick Starling (NC), Steve Steele (MD), Carl Stewart (NC), Gary Stewart (OR), Andy Stoll (IA), Mike Stolte (Canada), Erin Stone (OR), Bob Stott (England), Abby Straus (PA), Wendall Strode (KY), Wilma Strohmeier (ID), Susanne Sartelle (NC), Susan Wilson (KY), Rod Swink (NC), Cliff Swoape (TN), Gary Sycalik (CO), Bob Theobald (WA), Donna Thigpen (ND), Lauri Thomas (TX), Ron Thomas (GA), Chris Thomson (Spain), Steve Thornburg (NC), Parks Todd (NC), Charmaine Tomczyk (SC),

Margaret Thompkins (SC), Tom Tuttle (MD), Dr. Bob Tyndall (NC), Anne Udall (NC), Jack Uldrich (MI), Cathi Uldrich (NC), David Underbrink (TX), Dr. Jim Underwood (IL), Bob Utsman (NC), John Vanston (TX), Bob Veilleux (PA), Jim Villiesse (WI), Danielle Vorhees (MI), Niki Knox Vanderslice (GA), Dr. Keith Wade (FL), Susan Walker (MS), Zhihe Wang (China), Tim Ward (DC), Arthur Warmoth (CA), Anna Warth (AZ), Mark Waterhouse (CT), Barbara Weathers (MO), Randy Weaver (GA), Sherri Weidman (IN), Lee Weimer (CA), Yoram Weis (NC), Don Wells (NC), Jerry Wells (KY), Larry Wenzl (NE), Bob West (GA), Bill Whiland (Scotland), Paul Wildman (Australia), David Williams (NC), Randy Williams (TX), Bob Williford (NC), Bob Wilson (MS), Jean Gaddy Wilson (MO), Patricia Wilson (TX), Gabrielle Worth (SC), Alex Wojcicki (NC), Angie Woodward (KY), John Woolley (CA), Richard Worsley (England), Kristin Wreggitt (Canada), Jan Wright (Canada), Rob Youngblood (SC), Amy Zalman (DC), Steve Zeisler (DE),

Foreword

Community leaders everywhere are on the front lines of transformational changes and need to become pioneers in creating the communities of future we need.

Today the United States and the world are in a time of major structural changes – a turning point – with significant imbalances and instability, widespread confusion and conflicts, as well as opportunities and new frontiers. The directions of change and goals are being adopted by the international community, especially sustainable development and climate change goals and targets; nations are working on defining their contributions and strategies; those fearing change are marshalling resistance, some using violence; and greedy, corrupt and criminal groups are taking advantage of the situation. The great enablers of progress – education, energy, and science – are all in need of large scale change themselves to support pioneering work. Our justice and policing institutions need the capabilities to contain the enduring conflicts, large scale criminality, and deeply entrenched corruption that are huge impediments to the systemic changes we need. In addition, our governance systems were designed for an earlier era and must be modernized and streamlined to support robust governance operational, reform and transformation agendas globally, regionally, nationally and especially locally.

While goal setting is being done at the international and national levels, implementation is almost entirely local. It is communities where real action and change takes place. In the United States we have about 3,000 counties and more 35,000 municipalities. The Federal government's functions are almost entirely military and diplomacy and financial services (moving money around). Social services, education, economic development and environmental management are almost entirely community functions. State governments are in the middle doing their best to coordinate. Thus the front lines of transformation changes are our communities and their leadership.

The Communities of the Future network was created as a robust community of practice to focus on this need for building community transformational leadership capacity. I have had the pleasure of supporting Communities of the Future from its beginning in 1989. Rick Smyre and other community leaders were confronting the impacts of globalization and technological changes on communities that were losing their industries and identity and had to invent a new future for themselves. Over the years, the Communities of the Future network has learned by doing and sharing ideas and practices and accumulating a body of knowledge which is summarized in this valuable book with the contemporary challenge captured in its title: *Preparing for a World That Doesn't Exist-Yet: Framing a Second Enlightenment for the Communities of the Future.*

Today I am pleased to be engaged with Communities of the Future in charting its own future to mobilize its talent and knowledge to support community transformation through this turning point and to create the community governance capabilities we need to navigate the frontiers of the 21st Century and lay the foundation for 22nd Century governance. The transformational concepts and capabilities include Creative Molecular Economy, Transformational Learning/Future Forward College, Mobile Collaborative Governance, Master Capacity Builders, and the rise of a Second Enlightenment.

This book and the network of practitioners supporting its ideas and their implementation are a critical resource for community leaders everywhere. I commend Rick Smyre and Neil Richardson for both compiling the results of the Communities of the Future's work in this book and in mobilizing the network for the next generation of community transformational change.

Ken Hunter
Chairman, Senior Fellow Maryland China Initiative
University of Maryland

Past Chairman & Treasurer
World Future Society

Prologue

We are living on the precipice of a new era in human history. There is a new type of society emerging that Dr. John Cobb calls the Ecological Civilization. It is evolving, becoming more of a reality every day. This book is about how to prepare your community for this very different kind of society and economy. Whereas change historically has come from the top down, we believe that developing new capacities in local communities will transform not only our own daily lives, but the lives of everyone and everything on the planet. The planet is under multiple ecological and economic pressures, making it difficult to thrive and adapt to constant change. The issues of population growth, global warming, economic transformation, and loss of biological diversity are all interrelated for the first time in human history. As a result, traditional ideas and old models have become obsolete.

This book offers a new approach for an emerging society that will be increasingly fast-paced, interconnected, interdependent and complex. As a result, we will need to embrace interdependence, deep collaboration, connected individuality and nonlinear thinking and above all ... action in order to build new capacities for transformation that allow our communities to transform – moving from the ideas and methods of an Industrial Age to ideas and methods that will be aligned with a new Ecological Civilization.

Planning for a different kind of society and economy will require us to have an understanding of the past, yet to be defined by a vision focused on the future. Communities and organizations requiring fundamental change will need to approach the present and the future with an open mind. From this new, 21st century mind, we will be able to engage with and adapt to complexity using a lense capable of identifying the "weak signals" of ongoing transformation. We can understand the past, struggle with present issues, and simultaneously build parallel processes that allow new concepts and methods to emerge.

You never change things by fighting the existing reality. To change something, build a new model that makes the old model obsolete.
Buckminster Fuller

The science of complexity will emerge as key to the sustainability of a society in constant change because the future vitality of an Ecological Civilization relies on individual identity, culture, and social and economic systems that will be centered on biological principles, and not the traditional principles of physics.

This book is not about incremental change. It is a call to action among diverse people and organizations that will need to learn to collaborate and create capacities for transformation to be able to adapt to challenges that are emerging, but do not exist, yet. Reform does not fundamentally change anything. More often, reform prolongs problems and issues by masking an impending crisis within the context of a conventional strategic plan and standard performance metrics required in the Industrial Age filter of reality. Methods of reforming as a path to change do not work well as we enter an interconnected and interdependent Ecological Age. *Our society is faced with nothing less than creating something original … free of old ideas and mistakes of the past.*

Transformation is different from reformation in that it challenges the underlying assumptions of how we think about economic development, education, governance, and leadership. True transformation requires a clear mind: a mind that is observing our world, but not trying to control reality or leaping to quick conclusions. One of the recommendations we make is to be better connected; better connected to emerging innovative ideas, people and processes. Better connected by building deeper relationships within the community or organization we are serving to create an opportunity to stretch ourselves mentally and emotionally, in order to realize fully how aspirations, talent, vision and a total human being are engaged in design and fulfillment of transformational processes.

Transforming a community requires a core group of people who believe that this kind of transformational change is possible. A community can be as small as a group of neighbors aspiring to start a community garden on vacant land, or as big as a city rejuvenating after decades of decline or even an international collaboration of diverse people intent on creating a creative innovation ecosystem. Transforming any community, whatever its size, has repercussions that spread far beyond the initial objective and have far ranging impacts.

In an age where so many things regarding the planet seem to hang in the balance, the more people who become intentional about community transformation the better. As an example, one neighborhood garden can provide more nutritional food for people to lead healthier lives. By changing the way people eat, it can reduce the numbers of people who have diabetes or who are obese. When other neighborhoods follow suit, the initial garden becomes a catalyzing agent, like a tree spreading its seeds far and wide helps shape an ecosystem.

When someone who wants to learn to surf first begins surfing, it seems like a linear process. "If I practice this, I will do that," reflective of the linear approach of cause and effect. This does not turn out to be how it works at all. To be good at a complex activity like surfing requires someone to be highly adaptive. The water is different each day, the wind, the weather, the surfer's body are different every day also, and while there are funda-mental skills like standing on a particular spot of the board and knowing how to lean into the wave, that is not what makes a great or even a good surfer. The good and great surfers are adapting to what we call "felt unknowns," including the direction of the tide and wind, the variances of tide currents, and how their body is feeling. Any new surfer can stand upright for a long time without these sensitivities, but can only become good when shifting from a linear "all I need is the skills" approach to a non-linear, adaptive learning style that is responsive to unanticipated surprises. Making radical and transformational change requires engaging the unknown. To engage the unknown at a deep level, we have to approach issues free of the dependence on prediction and certainty. Otherwise, we are simply recycling what we know and trying to make old ideas and methods more efficient. Being comfortable with uncertainty and ambiguity long enough to allow creativity to emerge is a fundamental challenge for community change practitioners who are often bound to an election cycle or a traditional strategic plan.

In the United States, the founders accomplished great things by establishing the first true (if imperfect) democracy since the Ancient Greeks 2500 years ago. Over the two centuries since the United States was founded, it has spawned an amazing amount of innovation and created some of the greatest entrepreneurs in human history. From the end of World War II until the new millennium, the United States has been a core dominant force in nearly every important economic or cultural realm worldwide. In the last 30 years, the world has changed dramatically and will continue to do so. Partly due to globalization and partly due to the spread of technological innovation – especially the Internet – we now exist in a far more connected world than at any other time in human history. As a result, we can learn about things in real time that would have taken the greatest thinkers of antiquity years to find in a library.

In addition, more people are becoming part of a consumer culture of excess that leads to ever increasing amounts of carbon dioxide released into the atmosphere with the burning of fossil fuels. We, all of us, have a direct impact on how food is produced, energy is consumed, and national policy is engaged. Each dollar we spend on a consumer good or donated to a community based, non-governmental organization can have an exponential impact. Much like the compound interest of money, our activities are part of catalytic interlocking networks operating in even larger ecosystems, where connections explode like fireworks.

These connections are essential to understanding the creative innovation ecosystems on which this book is built. Arthur Koestler coined the term "holon" in his book *The Ghost in the Machine*, which is among the fundamental building blocks of this book. Every single thing is simultaneously whole and part of some other larger whole. When viewed in this way, everything is part of something else and all of those things make up an ecosystem.

This paragraph is made up of sentences, words and letters. The earth is made up of atoms, molecules, water, air, sand, mountain, continent, and planet ... and on and on it goes. In an Ecological Civilization, it is vital that people think and behave in deep and wide connected contexts, thinking in whole paragraphs, or seeing the Earth as a whole. We call this Holistic Thinking. In the West especially, science rules and events that are not observable are often denigrated as not actually real. We believe there are important things in the universe that are not observable, like love, mind and soul-ideas and attributes that will be key to the vitality and sustainability of an interconnected and interdependent society and economy.

A Master Capacity Builder is an individual who understands the precepts in this book and uses the ideas and methods to design and facilitate effective transformational processes at the community and organizational levels. An effective Master Capacity Builder must be able to process a wide variety of information and see how things connect while also being open to spontaneous new possibilities as they emerge. Many traditional planning processes are based on an extension of past best practices borrowed from other organizations and communities.

Too often we try to "fix" existing problems with existing and limited resources without concern for how the society and economy are transforming. As a result, there is an increased level of frustration as we try to make increasingly obsolete ideas and methods more efficient. Traditional strategic planning processes rarely work in a time of constant change, and are a big reason why long lasting and effective changes rarely happen. If we are to create a truly sustainable civilization as a result of transforming institutions and cities, we must see connections and tackle challenges with fresh ideas and an open and visionary mind; otherwise we will be doing little more than re-arranging deck chairs on a sinking Titanic.

When people are asked what defines the United States, invariably they will answer: "freedom and democracy." Freedom emphasizes our individual liberty, and democracy is the system whereby we govern ourselves together. The founders expected citizens to balance serving their own individual interests with serving the country. While our democracy has never been perfect, it has continued to evolve. The last twenty years have seen substantial conflict between conservatives and progressives. Moderates from both parties have found it difficult to stay in office and angry factions influence what Congress and the President can accomplish. Common ground is difficult to find and compromise is seen as a weakness. The influence of special interests and funneling of nearly unlimited amounts of money into campaigns and PACs have changed the face of democracy in the United State and represents a very different reality from what the founders could ever have imagined.

We believe that our democracy and institutions are no longer designed to be able to meet the challenges of an emerging society that will be very different from the past. We live in a time when, as identified by the World Economic Forum's Global Risks Report of 2012, we need to "re-conceptualize" all of society's institutions. We need different processes, concepts and methods created in local communities to help design and facilitate the transformation needed to birth a new type of society and economy that will be vital and sustainable in a time of exponential change. Citizens want to see their aspirations and hopes reflected in government policy at all levels. We believe that future leaders can facilitate broadened citizen engagement processes for community transformation by using the ideas and methods conveyed in this book.

We also believe that with new and creative processes, we can devolve government more effectively, shifting important decisions from Washington to our states and local communities. One of the most profound shifts we are recommending is recognizing the notion that in a time of constant change that leads to more complexity, our democracy needs to evolve beyond the concept of representative democracy that has served us so well for so long. This complexity requires a new approach, what we are calling Polycentric Democracy. At its core, Polycentric Democracy provides more direct ways for elected officials to access information and creative ideas from residents so that effective decision making processes can be developed and aligned with what a majority of citizens believe will be needed in the future. We call this new approach to decision making Mobile Collaborative Governance. Properly designed and facilitated, Mobile Collaborative Governance will offer opportunities for citizens to be in control of every phase of decision making for key issues in local communities. Such processes will require diverse groups of citizens working together on issues that are substantive and not refracted through the prism of party or ideology. We believe that Polycentric Democracy and Mobile Collaborative Governance will be an integral part of a system of community transformation in which a broad array of citizens can be involved in processes that make significant change occur in local communities. For this change to occur, a major effort will be required to seed knowledge of a different kind of emerging future in local communities. This will require nothing less than "comprehensive community transformation."

This book will introduce new concepts and methods we believe will be important to re-conceptualizing our economy and society. You will learn about transformational concepts such as Creative Molecular Economy, Transformational Learning/Future Forward College, Polycentric Democracy/Mobile Collaborative Governance, Master Capacity Builders and the rise of a Second Enlightenment. If you accept the premise of this book: that we are in a period of historical transformation requiring a Second Enlightenment, and that all traditional institutions need to be re-conceptualized, then each chapter of this book is a call to action for you to be part of growing number of voices working for true transformation.

Chapter 1

Emerging From the Mist: The Rise of a Second Enlightenment

A New Enlightenment

We are in a transition from an Industrial Society to an Ecological Civilization that will transform the fundamental principles of thinking and organization. Although it took 100 years for the First Enlightenment (1720–1820) to emerge, eventually a phrase appeared amongst the moderate thinkers of the time that personified the epoch. That phrase was "the new light," and the term Enlightenment became the historical way to capture the spirit of that age. Today's phrases, equally well known, are the "Space Age" and the "Information Age."

We live in an age of transformation where the concepts that grew out of the Enlightenment and undergirded the Industrial Age are evolving to a new worldview, complete with new fundamental principles, strategies and methods. No one is presumptuous enough at this stage in the historical transformation from one age to the next to think that all the key ideas and concepts can be identified, much less understood and applied. However, because the pace of change is faster and more complex than two hundred years ago, it is necessary for all citizens to begin to think about the implications of basic changes in our society. The change is occurring so fast that we know we are in some stage of transformation, which is different from what we read about previous changes. The universities and taverns of 18th century Scotland were havens of new thinking. Thinkers in those taverns and university salons felt pride and pleasure generating new ideas. One of our challenges is to create 21st century mechanisms, places, forums that will allow us to take enough time to ponder, talk, and ideate about transformational ideas just as did those participating in the coteries in Edinburgh in the 18th century.

We know many of the old ways of thinking already no longer work. Linear thinking grows more limited in a nonlinear world where the use of the Internet provides a matrix of simultaneous connections and disconnections. The one best answer may still be appropriate for an engineering equation, but not for the needs and capacities of a community in transformation. And, what about the capacity to innovate for increased income opportunities? We need to escape the search for standard solutions in order to innovate by seeing diverse connections among disparate ideas.

Rethinking the Obvious – What is Practical and Conservative in a Changing Society

We live in a time of such transformation that the basic ideas and principles that were successful in the past are no longer useful.

By analyzing the following traditional ideas from a perspective of the future, it becomes obvious why they are increasingly less useful:

- Let's do what is practical.
- We need to be conservative to insure the value of what we do.
- Let's decide what we want in the future and plan for it.

Let's do what is practical:

As Einstein said, "one cannot solve new problems with old ways of thinking." What is considered to be practical today was a radical idea sometime in the past … and traditional ideas are cracking as they always have in a time of historical transition.

We need to be conservative to maintain the value of what we have:

Conservatism is defined as the "disposition to preserve what is established." If an established organization, community and society wants to maintain vitality and sustainability when conditions and context within which each exists change, the most conservative thing to do is to change to insure survival. This is counterintuitive, and it necessitates new ideas in a process of what we call a "futures generative dialogue."

Let's decide what we want in the future and plan for it:

This is the basis for strategic planning. Change is occurring so fast we cannot predict the future. The best we can do is search for trends, weak signals and dialogue about what impact those trends may have. If you were a local economic developer in 1985, a mimeographed newsletter would still be used without realizing that the Internet had been in existence since 1969, and was getting ready to burst into the public consciousness around 1993 once the graphical interface of the Web was developed that allowed people and organizations in the public domain to communicate with one another in varied ways and in real time.

If we think about this implication for the future of our society, we begin to realize that we need to be able to think differently. We need to find connections where none apparently exist from a traditional perpective. We need to look for potential impacts of weak signals (what we call early signs of change) before they create a crisis. We need to think beyond the norm and realize that our context is constantly changing. How we see the world is different from how others see it. How we see the world in ten years will be different from how we see it today. We are facing a dynamic society of constant change while still trying to use the tools of a bygone age.

The significant problems we face today cannot be solved at the same level of thinking we used when we created them.
Albert Einstein

What can we do to prepare our communities and society for a different kind of future? We would suggest a counterintuitive idea. Before we "do" anything, we need to think about what we need to do. Think about how identifying emerging trends and weak signals could impact any new plan for the future. We need to build pools of leaders who can think about the future using principles, concepts, methods and techniques appropriate to a society in constant change that is interconnected by technology and that is increasingly complex This pool of leaders will be interconnected by increasingly complex technology. For us to be able to *"do"* the right thing, we need to think about what the right thing *"is"* in a changing context. Because so many changes are happening at once, we need to change the very nature of the questions we ask. What are all the things we need to think about and do in parallel to each other to build the capacities for vital and sustainable communities?

Rethinking the Future ... Searching for an Appropriate Framework of Ideas

Everyone knows the future will be different from the past. What we are just beginning to understand is that the challenges of the 21st century will probably require a "different kind of different" ... a future filled with qualitative changes as well as quantitative changes, with new principles that define and organize our society ... with a set of values that are adapted to meet the needs of a constantly changing context.

I first came to the realization that our society was in the early stages of immense transformation as a result of an experience I had in the textile industry in the mid-70s while CEO of a family controlled yarn spinning firm. 1974-75 was a major recession in the U.S. and was, for the textile industry, a mini-depression.

After World War Two, every six-seven years there was a limited recession of six months. Because interest rates were so low, it was standard procedure to continue to run the plants and build up inventory in order to keep the stability of the firm and especially the work force. The 1974-75 recession lasted eighteen months before the market returned to normalcy.

Something happened during this recession which was my first experience with a weak signal. However, my lens or filter of interpreting reality was not able to pick up the weak signal because of my training and the traditions of the textile industry. It was not until two years after the recession that I had an "aha" moment that would not only impact our textile firm, but also, over time, cause me to see the situation as a metaphor for the ongoing transformation of our society and economy.

Although no longer in existence, in 1970-80, Burlington Industries was the most well-known textile firm in the world. Based in Greensboro, NC, Burlington was the largest producer of woven fabrics of all kinds. The yarn that Burlington made was consumed by other divisions of the company as a part of a vertically integrated company. Our yarns were sold to the independent knitting industry throughout the U.S. Yarns that went into knitted fabrics had to be a better quality than those that went into woven goods that were made on a loom. Defects in woven yarns were not readily seen since the yarns were packed together due to the nature of how woven goods are constructed.

During times of recession after the Second World War, the demand for all goods was reduced, especially woven goods. In order to keep the stability of production for their many plants, Burlington had to find other markets for their yarns and sold a significant amount of their yarn production into the knitting goods area. To do this, Burlington had to reduce the price of their yarns by 50% so they could cover their fixed cost.

That is, Burlington did this for all recessions until the 1974-75 recession. In 1975 Burlington sold a yarn into the knitting market whose quality was better than the general quality of the spinners of knitting yarns … and at a price equal to our firms yarn. I remember calling a colleague of mine in the yarn spinning business and asked the question, 'George, have you heard about this new yarn that Burlington is selling in our market?' My next question reflected my lens or filter of reality in the textile industry. 'Where did Burlington get their source of Mississippi cotton that we do not have?'

I fully expected Burlington to withdraw their yarn from our knitting market after the recession was over. In fact, they expanded their production and the quality improved. For two years, I asked the same question, 'how can Burlington find a better grade of cotton than we can?' When the third year arrived and Burlington continued to sell a better quality of yarn than any firm in the knitting business did, I asked a different kind of question, 'what is Burlington doing that we are not doing?'

In asking a different type of question, I no longer made an assumption based on past experience of our industry. Over the next five months I found out that in 1970 Burlington had approached a U.S. Textile Machinery Manufacturer to transform the way cotton fiber was opened in the initial process of yarn spinning. Over one hundred years, a big, room-filling mechanical machine called a "picker" was standard for all yarn manufacturers. Burlington had the vision to realize that a new type of opening equipment could be designed based on new electronic methods and not mechanical principles.

When the U.S. Machinery Manufacturer expressed no interest in research and development to design a new type of opening equipment, Burlington approached a German manufacturer and spent four years from 1970-74 developing the idea of "electronic opening" which was the reason that the quality of Burlington's yarn in 1975 was better than ours.

From that point in the early 1970s, the paradigm of yarn spinning was transformed. It didn't matter whether we bought new pickers, added skills to the fixers of the pickers or changed the maintenance schedule for pickers. No matter what we could have done, we would not have been competitive unless we replaced the traditional pickers with "electronic opening" equipment.

Ten years later as I became fascinated with the ongoing changes in our society and economy, it hit me that if I had been receptive to new ways of thinking about transforming textiles methods, I would have asked a different kind of question more quickly and made a faster decision to buy electronic opening equipment.

I use this story as a metaphor for our society and economy. In many ways, leaders in local communities are using an out of date lens/filter to interpret and make decisions for the future without understanding that the context is changing. Too many local leaders either use a traditional filter to prepare for the future, or try to make ideas and methods that already exist more efficient … which is the definition of reforming change, not transformational change.

It was this personal experience that led me to begin to think about the present and future in very different ways as I read books and articles by visionary authors, and as I began to see the value to search out others who were very different in their thinking. This book is about the need to transform and reconceptualize all our traditional institutions, concepts and structures to be able to align with a society and economy in constant change. If each of you look back in your own professional life, you will find your "picker" story of transformation.

With this in mind, we need a new philosophic framework aligned with a society in exponential change. The following offers a framework that attempts to identify a basic shift of principles and ideas that may eventually be seen as important to 21st century society. At best, it is a partial list. Some of these ideas and principles may be seen as quickly obsolete or even irrelevant for the future. However, we are not concerned about rightness at this point, we are concerned about searching for a new way to think about and see the world. We are also concerned about how we prepare ourselves and our communities to function and be vital within a new type of society and economy. Over the last two centuries, it has been sufficient to reform the original ideas of the First Enlightenment. We have continuously improved basic ideas that have stood for more than two hundred years.

The ongoing transformation of our society will be based on different ideas and principles that are just beginning to emerge. As a result, we need to rethink old ideas and search for a Second Enlightenment. This Second Enlightenment needs to reflect the nature of our times as the previous First Enlightenment reflected the needs of the 18th and 19th centuries.

This framework below is designed in a different way. Not only does it attempt to identify the shift of ideas from one age to the next, but it also provides a column to reflect on how both ideas will be a part of the future. There is no right and wrong in these lists, only the best guesses of colleagues associated with the Second Enlightenment Project and the Center for Communities of the Future who have been thinking about transformation in our society for three decades. A key interest is how weak signals and trends will impact each other to create constantly changing contexts for the future. As you think about these ideas, select those most important to your organization and community, be open to all the ideas, and keep track of questions if you don't understand. They may be answered later in the book and if not, then they may contribute to the evolution of our ideas.

Living System Concepts for a Second Enlightenment

Consider the following core ideas as norms for each different age. The third column reflects the fact that both ideas in the first two columns will play appropriate roles over the next half-century, often at the same time in parallel with each other. However, over time, there will be a shift of emphasis from old to new principles. The story here is not that these earlier concepts were wrong, instead their truth was such that evolution reveals itself through adaptation.

First Enlightenment	Second Enlightenment	Ecological Civilization
Independent (either/or)	Interdependent (and/both)	Systemic Ecosystems
Self-interest	Help Each Other Succeed	Concomitant Good
Linear Thinking	Connective Thinking	Synthesis & Generation
Static Structures	Modules, Webs and Networks	Dynamic Adaptability
Reductionism	Holism	Connective Analysis
Standard Education & Accountability	Unlearning, Uplearning & Non-linear	Transformative Learning
Meaning from Materialism	Meaning from Creativity/Spiritualism	Balance of Values

Competition	Collaboration	Generative Development
Prediction and Certainty	Anticipation and Ambiguity	Parallel, Strategic and Adaptive Planning
Culture Dumbed Down	Culture Constantly Upgraded	Elegance in Complexity
Mix of Goodness and Skepticism	Integration of Reason and Mystery	Truth and Discovery Coexistent
Debate	Dialogue	Futures Generative Dialogue
One Best Answer	Choices	Concept of Applied Appropriateness
Representative Democracy	Electronic Republic	Polycentric Democracy/ Mobile Collaborative Governance

Understanding the Genetic Structure of a Dynamic Society

One of the challenges of creating a Second Enlightenment framework is the need to take the time to understand the potential transformation of basic assumptions that is emerging as the society changes. It is as if we were civil engineers trained in concepts of scaffolding, who are now asked to become evolutionary biologists, seeking to understand how new patterns of a dynamic society are emerging. Many of the old assumptions which reflect standard ways of looking at the world are no longer appropriate for a world in constant change.

This section seeks to take each major shift in thinking identified as Living Systems Concepts, provide definitions and offer an example of how each idea will be important in the 21st Century. When the book is finished, you will have a clear understanding of what we mean when we say that a new paradigm is emerging that will transform yourself, your field and our world.

For clarity we believe it is important to define what we mean for each concept. The reader can either work their way through these definitions one at a time, or refer back to them as you encounter them in the book. We do recommend that you be mindful of the Ecological Civilization concepts as they are emergent.

Principle One: Independent, Interdependent, Systemic

Independent

The idea of individuals having the capability of being sovereign and having worth in and of themselves was a new idea that developed a tipping point of acceptance in the 18th century. When connected to the idea that people could have a direct relationship with God without the intercession of a priest (leading to literacy, democracy, and classical liberalism), independence became an important principle for the Enlightenment society. Over the years, the original concept of individual rights has lost the idea of responsibility that served as the glue of community. We live in a time of radical individualism in the United States and other Western countries where the market and democracy have taken root. As a result, not only are we losing bonds of connectedness, we are thrown into a cultural conflict as the interacting patterns of our society and the world increasingly require interdependent concepts and methods.

Interdependent

Today the context of our society is transforming and we are seeing a society emerge that is so fast-paced and technically interconnected, that it has become increasingly interdependent. Some will say, "we have always been interdependent" and they would be correct. However, we could always escape physical and psychological nearness if necessary. We could always move "West," geographically or theoretically, and find an environment which fostered independence. However, increasingly we live among diverse people and more of them. Our world economy is connected by greater trade and larger, faster financial flows. Even our ability to vote and eat is interdependent with technology. In an increasingly interdependent and complex world, *we will need to help each other succeed.*

Systemic

As all facets of life become more interdependent, we will need to function to a much greater extent in connected ways. An Ecological Civilization will see major shifts in all aspects of our social, political, educational, cultural and scientific systems at the same time that our concept of interdependence evolves. We will shift from emphasizing the unconscious ego need to be self-sufficient, to focus on the need to connect with others in a process of discovery and idea generation. At the same time we will need to be self-reliant and, at times, "do for ourselves." In the future, it will no longer be either/or, it will be "and/both."

An Example – Principle 1

As economic developers increasingly recognize the shift of

employment from manufacturing to knowledge entrepreneurs, there will be a need for entrepreneurs to learn how to build individual income streams using individually distinctive knowledge in connection with electronic entrepreneurial teams. We call this a "creative innovation ecosystem." As a result, it will be necessary for individuals to emphasize their own need for broader and deeper learning at the same time that they connect with other people anywhere in the world to link the values of their individual capacities, knowledge and talents. In other words, the idea of integrating individual independence and team interdependence into a comprehensive capacity of the whole (systemic ecosystems) will become the norm. It will be characteristic of a Creative Ecological Civilization.

Principle Two: Self-Interest, Help Each Other Succeed, Concomitant Good

Self-Interest

One of the most identifiable ideas of a democratic and capitalist society is the concept of self-interest. "Self-interest, rightly understood," Tocqueville said, is the basis for the success of community in the American society. The original concept of civil society is based on the idea that individuals will reach out to others as a result of their own self-interest. This has been true as long as the values of the 18th century emphasized the need to have a morality that prevented individual self-interest from becoming selfishness. The original concept of self-interest was based on an understanding of the need for individuals to help promote the common good because no individual lives in a vacuum.

Help Each Other Succeed

As society, and the world, becomes more connected and the complexity of issues moves beyond the capability of any one group, community or nation to work alone, there is an increasing need to collaborate and help each other succeed. This need has already existed for years. However, only now are we beginning to realize that we have reached a threshold where deep collaboration is essential most of the time. We are at a point in the struggle for sustainability where "helping each other succeed" will become a slogan of the times. The capacity and methods of collaboration will require the use of judgment. We will need to trust those with whom we work, even those we don't know, until they show they can't be trusted. This need for deeper trust is an impact of the fast pace of change that we have not yet fully discerned. It should also be noted that self-interest has evolved from the founders' idealisitic notion of an individual acting in relation to the common good to a highly individualistic version influenced by Friedrich Nietzsche and Ayn Rand's Objectivisim beginning in the late 19th century and into the 20th century. The wheel of change is bringing us forward to a more integrated understanding that people at their core are interrelated.

Concomitant Good

In a constantly changing, interdependent society, one has to think about the interrelationship of the individual to the whole at all times. One's individual action will impact other people either directly (short run action) or indirectly (longer time it takes to make the impact of a new decision or action felt). The idea of a concomitant good replaces the idea of common good. Common good was used to represent taking the collective community into consideration and, usually, represented some decision made on the part of an elected body that was to give the greatest good to the greatest number. Concomitant good is a step up in understanding that there is a need for *an individual and group* to consider the impact of their actions and decisions on the context of the situation. In turn, any change in the context that occurs will impact the individual and or group. There increasingly exists a need to look at the whole and to consider multiple factors when deciding what strategy to use and what action to take. As a result, each individual will begin to need to think about multiple "concomitant goods" that are interactive and need to balance appropriate self-interest with helping others to succeed. With this in mind, individual meaning will be found in the act of collaborating with others to help create and build a viable and sustainable Ecological Civilization.

An Example – Principle 2

David Hume and his followers in the Scottish Enlightenment made the assumption that people acted out of habit, not because they rationally wanted to improve the lot of their fellow man. He was a skeptic in a time of historical transformation. It is our challenge to find ways to connect diverse people where they work as individuals and communities for "concomitant good." A good example is the need for local political leaders to understand that, in a constantly changing society, an important role of leadership will be to build new capacities to help broaden the ability of local citizens to take control of their own lives and generate new ideas for the good of the community. Local leaders will need to develop the capacity to design new processes which will help bring interested citizens together to generate transformational ideas. For example, leadership in a local community could decide to design and implement a new economic development project using "community cash" to network participating businesses to create a local currency to add to traditional demand for goods and services. Assuming positive results, the media might pick up the success and promote it in other areas. Hearing of this "creative community," other young professional knowledge workers might locate there and add to the success of the community. The result of a diversity of small projects could change the context of the community with the resulting enhancement and growth overall of transformational ideas. A perfect example of developing an environment for the "concomitant good."

Principle 3: Linear Thinking, Connective Thinking, Synthesis & Generation

Linear Thinking

When we ask for the "bottom line," very rarely do we mean more than to go ahead and give the one answer that will solve the problem. This is the effect of the First Enlightenment on our thinking. When crises exist, a focus on immediate outcomes is needed. When someone needs a heart operation, the linear methods of past scientific experiments provide the building blocks of today's success. Our traditional manufacturing methods are the result of getting the best product or service that money can buy. This principle of linearity has been on target as long as standardized models and singular actions were appropriate and reached its apex with the mechanistic mindset in the post war years. With the development of government bureaucracies based on skillsets instead of patronage beginning in the early 20th century and the large centralized systems that were a response to the needs of World War II, there was a moment in time when linearity was seen as the culmination of modernity and efficiency. However, with increased change and the need for continuous innovation and continuous transformation, the one best way and linear thinking needs to be complemented.

Connective Thinking

When life speeds up, we run into more situations where we need to understand how things connect. New ideas create innovations and keep our income flowing and our economy strong. Law enforcement uses technology to discover and uncover criminals using computer simulations and connective analysis. Seeing patterns in apparent chaos offers a way to stop the spread of raging disease among continents. The capacity to analyze complex issues offers leaders the opportunity to make our democracy more vibrant and rich. A central feature of these examples is the ability for those involved to be connective thinkers. In the 21st century, the most important function of education will be to create students who can both identify and spawn connections.

Synthesis, Generation and Parallel Processes

Connective thinking, in combination with processes of generative dialogue, leads to synthesis and new ideas. The very nature of seeing new connections is the basis for continuous innovations and continuous transformation. Once a new idea is developed using connective thinking, new strategies become important to implement the idea. This requires a combination of non-linear, connective thinking to build effective parallel processes, and linear thinking to make sure effective actions are taken with accountable outcomes defined. A constantly changing society will require leaders to become proficient in both linear, cause and effect thinking, and non-linear, connective thinking, and be able to use both when appropriate. The matrix for understanding an issue in totality is to see it from the most perspectives possible.

An Example: Principle 3

The Tartan Transformation Project was conceived through connective and linear thinking. The basic idea is to have people of Scottish heritage in different parts of the U.S. and world become involved in thinking about the ways in which they could connect with Scotland at the same time that they worked with the Center for Communities of the Future to develop generative dialogue that would undergird the evolution of a framework of the Second Enlightenment ideas aligned with the emerging society. To this end, three project strands were conceived (nonlinear and linear) that would leverage each other. The first strand of the TTP is the idea of building a U.S.-Scottish relationship that would draw golfers and other tourists into the two countries as an economic development project (linear thinking). The second strand would focus on the development of small groups of people with Scottish heritage who would work together in local communities to dialogue about the Second Enlightenment concepts (linear/non-linear). They would also work to have local people become involved in economic development connections with associates in Scotland. The third strand requires connective thinking to: 1) understand the ideas of the Scottish Enlightenment, 2) think about trends of the future, 3) create "futures projects" that are as consistent with the emergence of today's society as were the ideas of the Scottish Enlightenment to the practical realities of the 18th century.

Principle Four: Static Structures, Modules, Webs & Interlocking Networks, Dynamic Adaptability

Static Structures

Adam Smith introduced the concept of specialization as a way to increase economic efficiency. One hundred and fifty years later, Fredrick Taylor introduced the idea of standardization. The combination of these two ideas created bureaucracy. The idea of specializing and standardizing also led to static structures where hierarchies are the dominant form and the "one best answer" is the norm. This led to resistance to change as all sectors of society looked to maximize existing ways of doing things. Even today, in a world of constant change, we define the success of education based on the results of standardized testing. Of course, there is value in standards where singular excellence is required, as long as the concept of what excellence is can be adapted within the context of any transformation. As a manufacturer, world-class standards are imperative to compete in an international economy. However, if the methods, technology or concepts of management are static and incapable of adapting to changing circumstances, failure will result at some time. In the future failure will come faster and faster for those who cannot adapt, whether an individual, a business, or a community. Just consider how the advent of rapid prototyping and 3-D manufacturing is transforming the very nature of the concept of manufacturing. It won't be long before individualized manufacturing is done in one's home.

Modules, Webs and Interlocking Networks

As the pace of change increases, tensions will increase and old structures break apart as if society were a bridge whose materials had worn out. Any student of biology learns that as systems become more complex, "webs of intricacy" are formed by connecting small units together in appropriate ways. Our very bodies evolve by the connections of diverse cells and interaction of proteins, sugars and more complex compounds. Our societies are emerging in similar ways. As population increases and the Internet connects a diversity of people and ideas throughout the world, the use of webs and networks is quickly becoming the building block of social and economy activity. It is predicted that in twenty years, the largest economic corporation will have a core nucleus of five hundred to fifteen hundred facilitators, and the rest of the organization will be brought together and broken apart as required, whether for research and development, contracted production or electronic marketing. As the concept of standard education is shifted to one of Transformational Learning, core modules of knowledge will be stitched together within a futures context as required. This will allow all human, economic and learning systems to have dynamic adaptability. Biological patterns indicate that things speed up, slow down and then die ... adaptation can create greater and longer sustainability.

Dynamic Adaptability

Of great significance in the future will be the need for individuals, organizations and communities to be able to develop the potential for dynamic adaptability. This will not occur without great struggle because the shift in capacities, values and knowledge bases that will be necessary is huge and daunting. Complex adaptive systems are maintained by the capacity to anticipate change and to develop skills, behaviors and attitudes consistent with an environment that continuously emerges. Electronic access to information is transforming the very nature of our governmental structures to foster the development of webs and networks, and allow decision making to be devolved to the lowest possible level. As the adaptability of governance increases, it will bring into question whether a system built on checks and balances is capable of adapting to the needs of a fast-paced society. The transformation of one area of society (e.g. technology and the Internet) will create an environment where other parts of the society will need to rethink their values and methods. It will be the "butterfly effect" multiplied by ten because one change in one part of the system will quickly impact other parts of the system. In the next decade it is said that we will reach a point where we are doubling human knowledge every half day and it will speed up from there.

An Example: Principle Four

Any organization and community that has not shifted from command and control to team and interlocking network structures will not be able to move quickly enough and with enough quality to compete in the marketplace. Whether the marketplace be one of products or ideas. The United Way faced the problem that as more and more manufacturing businesses automate or go out of business, there are smaller pools of workers from which to solicit donations. As a result many local United Ways are facing the need to rethink their organizational approach to funding their agencies. One of the more innovative approaches is to network neighborhoods and to connect smaller webs into larger webs. In addition, there is now the capacity to allow self-organizing networks of donors to provide ideas and funding at the same time for research and development projects. In so doing, these United Ways are reflecting the idea of "dynamic adaptability."

Principle Five: Reductionism, Holism, Connective Analysis

Reductionism

The Industrial Age was excellent at reducing everything to its smallest component part and then reassembling it into the whole. In so doing we reached, many of the greatest scientific achievements of history to date in the fields of Chemistry and Physics. We analyzed the natural order of the world and applied the principles to machines and other practical uses. The development of the steam engine and the dyeing of fabric directly resulted from reductionist methods. However, recent discoveries in biology, genetics and quantum physics have brought to light the need to think about things systemically or in the whole. It is called the nature of holism. What we know about the small world is still beautiful and true in its simplicity, but more connections mean more elegance in complexity and that means even more truth.

Holism and Holarcy

The increased complexity of society and other organisms requires the need to think about overall structures and properties and how they interact and interrelate. In Biology, the nature of proteins and glycosides are impacted by not just their constituent parts, but also by the shape of their holistic structures. In society, local leaders are beginning to realize that since their standard policies do not impact diverse ethnic groups in common ways, it is actually only through a greater diversity of thinking and action that any kind of unity is possible. As complexity emerges, the nature of how patterns are changed by the interaction of multiple factors requires thinking about the overall, holistic nature of any situation.

Connective Analysis

Think globally, act locally is a two-decades' old phrase that emphasizes the need for business people and economic developers to know what is happening in the world economy so that their local economic strategies can be more effective. There is the need to be able to see connections and analyze their potential impact on existing issues. Connective Analysis is the ability to see how apparently disparate factors can be connected to create a niche or new product category in business, or a new idea in society. City managers will need Connective Analysis as they try to understand the changes occurring in their communities. This mastery includes the ability to integrate the ideas of reducing complexities to understand how ecosystems are formed by connections, at the same time considering the overall system. Only by breaking apart and reconnecting appropriate strategies based on holistic, continuous feedback will Connective Analysis offer the opportunity to seed a community with new capacities for transformation. In essence, Connective Analysis is about deconstructing an issue and reassembling the pieces in such a way that allows for the transcendence of each high peak and the inclusion of each valley even with its challenges, so that what emerges incorporates the most truth possible.

An Example: Principle 5

One of the most important uses of Connective Analysis is the creation of a framework of thinking in any community that is focused on emerging trends and weak signals. A "futures context" is formed as specific actions are taken, and emerging issues are considered in relation to the needs of a society and economy that is interconnected, interdependent, and increasingly fast-paced and complex.

As an example, there is a new idea that is in its early stages of emerging in the Piedmont of North Carolina. The Chamber of Commerce in Statesville, NC is taking the leadership to develop a concept called "comprehensive community transformation" in collaboration with the Center for Communities of the Future. This idea is based on the need to reconceptualize all institutions in ways that will seed transformational ideas such as Master Capacity Builders, Future Forward College, Polycentric Democracy, and Creative Molecular Economy.

All of these ideas are based on the undergirding principle that local areas need to build parallel processes that seed "capacities for transformation" in the thinking and action of all citizens over time. With this in mind, a concept for Statesville has emerged to develop five parallel processes in which citizens can self-select to be involved that will create a culture open to totally new concepts of how people lead (Master Capacity Builders), how economic development is done (Creative Molecular Economy), how education and learning occurs (Transformational Learning) and how decisions are made through broadened citizen engagement (Polycentric Democracy and Mobile Collaborative Governance).

One of the unique features of Connective Analysis when designing systems of interlocking networks and parallel processes, is that there is no limitation in developing a strategy for any local area. In the case of Statesville, there is an evolving connection with other ongoing processes to include Davidson College, a group of Davidson graduates of the Class of '64 and other networks of people working in collaboration. Representatives from Statesville are also involved with a network of colleagues in North Carolina and other states who are collaborating with smaller communities under 25,000 residents. The objective of this network is to bring leaders from these communities together with colleagues from Statesville, COTF, economic development groups and Davidson to introduce futures thinking to local leaders of small communities who can then promote the idea of the impact of trends and weak signals indirectly to the citizens of their communities.

Thus, the idea of Connective Analysis opens up new possibilities by identifying access points to seed transformational thinking and action in the community, as well as by designing larger systems of interlocking networks and parallel processes in order to create a culture conducive to the initiation and evolution of "comprehensive community transformation."

Principle Six: Standard Education/Accountability, Unlearning and Uplearning, Transformational Learning

Standard Education/Accountability

The educational system in the United States is a product of Scottish and German influences. One emphasized the unity of knowledge and in-depth, liberal arts curricula, the other scientific reductionism of a curricula based on what is of interest or importance at the moment. Our society used economics and reductionist data analysis to create standardized curricula developed with accountability based on testing in narrow limits. Learning for overall meaning shifted to education for vocational training. This dichotomy, exemplified by true/false questions, has led to a dichotomy of seeing the world and limits our capacity to see connections and to dive beneath the surface of causal thinking. It prevents us from dealing with the nuances and subtleties of an increasingly complex world. We are now faced with a telling challenge to unlearn our traditional educational ideas and uplearn at a more complex level. Work in the future will tax the brain more than the body.

Unlearning & Uplearning

It is not that we are to cast away content of appropriate knowledge, it is that we need to unlearn many old "truths," one of which is that there is only one answer to all situations and issues. Once we learn how to unlearn inappropriate ideas and remove obsolete knowledge, we can learn how to uplearn, to think and act at a higher level of complexity. We ask for simplicity in a complex age, not realizing that what will be seen as simple by our grandchildren, we see as complex today. That is not new; it has been so throughout history. Have we come to believe that there is no honor in intellectual struggle? Are we so conditioned by manufacturing's need for shortening the cycle of production that we fail to realize that often patience is needed for new ideas to form? Are we so immobilized by the needs of an immediate 24/7 society, that we only want to live in a world of limited simplicity where there is little risk? Do we find no sense of pleasure looking for ways to enhance how people can think creatively without having an immediate answer? We have many challenges. None is more important than providing a safe environment where people are able to think differently without recrimination and without having to come to some immediate conclusion. We are faced with the need to transform our learning context as well as traditional learning methods.

Transformational Learning

The vitality of our future will be directly related to our ability to think within a futures context. The future of learning will require all citizens to become and/both, connective thinkers, able to see new patterns, leaving the world of "one best" answers *only* which often leads to debate about which truth is correct. Future trends are by nature imprecise because no one can predict the future. In our need to anticipate the future, the study of future trends is a must. Yet we must not stop there. Content of knowledge needs to be broadened and deepened to give people more capacity to be able to innovate – especially leaders in a democracy. To do this we need to focus on how to identify "weak signals" as they emerge, how to ask appropriate questions, and how to find connections in apparently disparate areas of knowledge and life. Systemic thinking can be introduced by multimedia which can give a visual representation to a new idea using virtual learning techniques. The nature of Transformational Learning is diverse and will require standards when necessary (manufacturing processes and world class healthcare) and uplearning, connective thinking when necessary. A framework of Transformational Learning will evolve that provides the skills for continuous transformation *and* aligns with the needs of a constantly changing society. It is imperative that we approach challenges with a fresh mind that is not held back by the old way of doing things.

An Example: Principle 6

A recent virtual conference in which we participated employed the concepts and methods of "transformational learning" for one of its courses. Those participating were given a resource list of websites, books and articles. Two questions were asked in advance and no one was told what to read. Each person began a dialogue with the "learning guide" and a "futures generative dialogue" ensued. Not only did each of the participants take control of their own learning experience, the route of learning could not be predicted or standardized as a result of the way the learning guide kept shifting the focus of the questions. In so doing, different methods of connective learning were demonstrated, often without the knowledge of the participants.

One of the results was that the "learning guide" ended up learning as much as did the participants, who reported that they learned a tremendous amount. This is the essence of "reciprocal learning," when we learn different things from each other during the same learning experience.

Principle Seven: Meaning from Materialism, Meaning from Creativity/Spiritualism, Balance of Values

Meaning from Materialism

One of the key shifts from the Renaissance to the Enlightenment was the opening of the door to secular thought. No longer was all meaning found only in religion, there was a reasonable role for man to play and have worth in and of himself. The concept of natural law came into play and it became legitimate for man, now we would say people, to build treasures on earth as well as in heaven. The impact of Scotland's intellectual leaders on day-to-day life was immense. As new tributaries of thought converged in the later part of the 18th century, the rise of the idea of individual rights and market opportunities created an environment where materialism was added to the stage of religious leaders. There was an "idea of light" that spread through Scottish society. As time progressed several thinkers coined the term "outward signs of inward grace" and the Western culture developed a sense that one's worth was based on one's material wealth.

No society can surely be flourishing and happy, when the far greater part of the members are poor and miserable. Adam Smith championed the concept of voluntary self-restraint, brought about by a personal commitment to moral responsibility. Societies that are able to function with a high degree of trust, brought about by shared moral precepts and the strong expectation that impulses of greed will be reasonably checked by self-control, will provide more agreeable conditions for the flouring of a free society with a limited government. Accordingly, greed is not the same as healthy self interest—not in our modern world, and not in the world of Adam Smith.

Jonathan B. Wright
Robins School of Business
University of Richmond

Meaning from Creativity/Spiritualism

The desire of people in poverty to have a better material life is balanced by the need of all countries to find meaning in working together to create a sustainable world. As we evolve to a more complex and changing network of interacting individuals and groups, there will be an increased need to care for each other and to find value in "acts of life" beyond the necessity to maximize the search for material wealth. In the 21st century, we expect meaning to come from the constant intersection of human creativity and spiritual commitment. As we rediscover a broader and deeper spirituality, we will find happiness reaching beyond selfish motives to offer one's talents for the "concomitant good." In so doing, enough individual material wealth will be gained, but not at the sacrifice of the moral, mental and spiritual health of the entire society. Leadership will grow in networks of diverse people who look for the value in what others say and do, without losing the essence of each person's own diversity. The new definition of maturity recognizes the internal role of religious faith and its inherent ambiguity connected to the external role of secular life. The shift will be to "uplearn" to a balance of values that sustain a dynamic society at the same time that "connected individuality" is deepened.

Balance of Values

One of the dramatic shifts undergirding our Western Societies is a search for ways to balance the need for environmental health, political freedom and material sustenance. We need to learn to think differently as well as a need to identify those values that will become important to sustainability. The ability to be a connected thinker will allow individuals to see the value in what others think and do without losing one's sense of self. This assumes that no individual has "the truth" and thus is always searching for meaning in new ideas that can be connected to existing opinions in order to become more flexible and resilient. To do so effectively we need to get beyond one-dimensional thinking. Looking for the one best answer means you cannot see value in the other's thoughts. One must "value" the ability to connect with other ideas as appropriate, and to do this, one must be open to new ideas. Only by being an "and/both" thinker will one be open to new ideas. Only if one is open to new ideas can one be sensitive to the thoughts of others and look for value in what others say. The following will need to be included in a foundation of values to support a context that has the capability to adapt to changing circumstances:

1) Connecting with others to help them succeed;
2) Recognizing the value of diversity and the fact that without diversity there is no growth and evolution to a higher order of thinking and acting;
3) Seeing creativity within a futures context as important to the continuous innovation necessary to have a sustainable and vital economy and society;
4) Seeing futures generative dialogue and thinking about new ideas as important;
5) Searching for an effective balance of human, moral, economic, spiritual and ethical values without dwelling on one as more dominant compared to the others.

Personal identity will come from collaborating with others to create solutions for emerging complex issues, and not from the traditional focus of money, power and control.

An Example: Principle 7

Twenty years ago, a study by Kruse and Blasi of Rutgers University found that companies that have an ESOP (employee stock ownership program) increase overall sales and sales per employee by 2.3% and 2.4%. They also have a better record of staying in business. So what, you may ask. There are other examples of where ESOPs didn't work. Both points are true. We are moving into an age where there will be multiple ideas and multiple methods to reach a goal. This example is one of the creativity of one man, Louis Kelso, in the search for a balance of values. Recognizing in early 1972 that economic efficiency and job satisfaction were both declining, Kelso approached Russell Long of the U.S. Senate to consider changing the tax laws to help companies be competitive, while, at the same time, creating an environment where associates could not only own a part of the company, but also be involved in decision making that fostered human and family values. Like this example, the future will require creativity in all parts of society to find new ways to balance economic, family, human, moral, spiritual and ethical values.

Principle 8: Competition, Collaboration, Generative Development

Competition

Only individual rights in our democracy are more sacred as a concept than the right to develop value through individual merit and not by birth. This idea quickly transferred to the economy and competition became the centerpiece of economic growth and health. However, we are in the age predicted by Adam Smith.

Smith predicted any market society could evolve into a time of greed and corruption where "money values" were emphasized to excess. Competition has a bright and dark side. When one competes to win, one is able to go beyond the limitations of the past, whether economically or a long distance runner. However, without moral values that limit cheating and winning at all costs, competition's dark side takes over. And we run the risk of being successful economically and politically without any morality or sense of meaning. A challenge of the future will be to compete and collaborate in creating a sustainable society and world, and doing it with balance that is fair and does not demonize the less successful.

Collaboration

In an interdependent community and society, traditional competition without regard to the impact on others will not only be injurious to the community but to ourselves as well. If we are selfish and care little for our neighbor, the old approach to competition will only cause harm because of the need to understand that in a more complex society, the multiplicities of needs are too large to be provided by one person or one organization. We can already see a weak signal indicating the need for deeper collaboration in the economic realm as firms compete and collaborate at the same time due to the need to access capital and talents beyond the scope of the individual firm. The same principle is true in education where virtual networks of talented people will collaborate to work as coaches in continuous learning experiences due to the complexity and shift in thinking from standard educational concepts to those of Transformational Learning.

There is a difference between collaboration and cooperation. Today, most people and organizations cooperate when it is to their self-interest and when individual goals and objectives have already been set. In the future, true collaboration will only occur when those involved sit and dialogue in ways that put themselves in the other person's place and, together, all involved help each other think through the issues of how to develop a set of mutual values, concepts, strategies and actions that are appropriate to the needs of the moment whether a short- or long-term need.

Generative Development

With competition and collaboration in mind, individuals and groups in the future will find the need to integrate the two concepts as a part of a new approach called generative development. Generative development assumes that creativity, sustainability and concern for ethics and morality are paramount. The goal of any process of generative development is to establish creative solutions to shorter- and longer-term needs in parallel. All the while thinking of how ideas and actions will be impacted by future trends. Without thinking in an immediate and futures context at the same time, there can be no generative development. Without the ability to listen and see some value in something that others are saying, there can be no connections to generate new ideas. Without a purpose that meets individual growth needs and community transformation needs at the same time, there can be no generative development for a community. Instead of winning at all costs, the focus of generative development is to find new ways to balance the needs of competing sectors of society, and, in so doing, create purpose for individuals and groups in mutual acts of creation.

An Example: Principle 8

A good example is the new "Paradigm Shift" project that is emerging at Wake Tech CC as a part of their Future Forward College concept. This project combines futures generative dialogue, networking, use of the Internet, transformative thinking and parallel processes. A core group 10-15 students is introduced to various websites on which they can find emerging trends and weak signals. This core group self-organizes into subgroups based on the selection of areas of interest. Each group creates a pilot transformational idea that can be introduced into the college and community, or designed as a business start up connected to different ecosystems as a result of the COTF Network that includes nationally known economic developers. In so doing, the learning experience moves beyond knowing content and requires students to be able to ask appropriate questions, connect disparate ideas and anticipate needs of the society that do not presently exist. As a result the paradigm of learning is shifted from content only to connecting diverse weak signals as a platform for creativity.

Principle 9: Prediction and Certainty, Anticipation & Ambiguity, Parallel Strategic and Ecological Planning

Prediction and Certainty

The search for scientific certainty came from the need to understand natural phenomena in the aftermath of religious corruption of the Middle Ages. Scottish thinkers expanded the search for certainty and combined it with practical technical applications to develop the first application of steam to meet industrial needs. As time evolved, prediction came to the forefront of social planning and natural laws were defined which could support a glimpse into the future as long as the same conditions using the consistent methods insured the same results, time after time. Western Society, especially the United States, has based its progress on prediction and control. Benchmarking and accountability are based on standards where outcomes repeat themselves. However, now that we are entering a time requiring continuous innovation and continuous transformation, the very mindset of predictability for all outcomes breaks down and the capacity to anticipate alternatives in a flood of uncertainty becomes a valuable capacity.

Anticipation and Ambiguity

When the context is fixed, one can anticipate without great uncertainty. Consider Wayne Gretsky, the Hall of Fame hockey player. He knew that the rink would not change its shape and was able to anticipate the puck better that anyone in the history of hockey. With a changing context, there are many more factors to consider. We need to develop the ability to be comfortable with ambiguity so that we are able to think about what interactions may occur and what different alternatives need to be considered. Those individuals who need the "one best answer" will need to connect themselves to a more stable profession such as accounting and manufacturing (before the majority of manufacturing becomes individualized with 3D printing within twenty years). Those who develop the capacity to anticipate the future and who are comfortable with uncertainty and ambiguity will be more predisposed to be involved with areas of life that will require continuous innovation. We need to change all of the fields of technology to draw these types of people through their doors. Early adopters will figure out that the more knowledge one has in all fields, the better off one is to be an innovator by seeing connections and patterns that others cannot see. The capacity to be a connective thinker will be imperative for success in a constantly changing and ambiguous world.

Parallel Strategic and Adaptive Planning

In an age of linear thinking and strategic planning, where the outcomes are defined before the process begins, and where our educational methods focus on the one best answer, it often appears that we need to choose either the method of prediction or becoming comfortable with uncertainty and ambiguity. In some cases this will be true. Preventive Health methods will continue to attempt to predict disease based on databases developed over time. The rarer the health condition, the more computer simulations and databases will be needed to add to diagnostic accuracy. In other fields, ambiguity will be more important. In the field of artificial intelligence, prediction is not useful as software learns to adapt to changing conditions. Planning is one area where the two ideas will work in parallel. If one is concerned about the short term and has resources and outcomes already defined, then strategic planning is appropriate. However, the longer the timeframe of planning, the more ambiguity will exist, and the more we need new techniques of anticipating uncertainty. If one looks twenty years ahead, one needs to look for weak signals before they become trends and to learn how to frame and seed the creation of new capacities that will help insure any organization or community will be able to transform itself. Again, we need the key capacity of seeing connections among apparently disparate factors. The ideas of biology and ecology also become important for the long term, and are the basis for the new field of adaptive planning. Instead of trying to identify specific outcomes at the beginning of any process, adaptive planning emphasizes the creation of small groups of committed people to study various trends and areas of community life and then begin to generate new ideas from the dialogue which ensues. Outcomes emerge from the futures generative dialogue.

An Example: Principle 9

Today, there are three economies in churn (mixed together and moving simultaneously) an Industrial Economy, a Knowledge Economy and the early stages of a Creative Molecular Economy. By the year 2025, we expect that 35-40% of all workers will be working out of their homes as electronic entrepreneurs. Since no one can predict the exact type of work that will be available in 2025, the best one can do is to establish parallel processes where jobs are developed locally as well as recruited from other areas. It is also important that we develop the capacity in all citizens to understand how to identify weak signals and emerging trends in order to build individual and community skills able to support a sustainable and viable economy in the future that will be based on networks of entrepreneurs. Therefore, any local economic developer needs to be a developer of parallel processes: strategic planning for the short run to target specific projects, and adaptive planning for the longer run to develop capacities appropriate for a transforming economy.

Principle 10: Culture Dumbed Down, Culture Constantly Upgraded, Elegance in Complexity

Culture Dumbed Down

We can see an existing tension in our egalitarian society. On the one hand, the political sphere emphasizes a language that speaks so all people can understand. On the other, the hypercompetitive nature of our worldwide economy is based on being different and distinctive on purpose. Add to this the increasingly complex nature of our international clash of civilizations, and it becomes obvious that dumbing down to be understood no longer works for us. When people are ridiculed as being nerds, they wonder why, because intellectuals will be in demand in a Creative Knowledge Economy and throughout the Ecological Civilization. And yet, at the same time, we find entertainment filled with violence and crudeness that has been dumbed down for cultural consumption. We make money into a god by marketing to sell to the desires of a less educated population. It is this dumbing down of culture that fails to prepare us for the future whether it be the dumbing down of our culture or of our morality. Our future vitality will require the need to upgrade the knowledge base and moral and ethical fiber of the population to think and act maturely at a higher level in order to be able to innovate and collaborate in sustainable ways.

Culture Constantly Upgraded

If we are to become prepared for an increasingly complex and interdependent society, we will need to upgrade our culture. Not only will we need to improve the knowledge base of individuals, we will need to develop the capacities of organizations and communities to adapt to the needs of a constantly changing society and economy. In each case, those involved will need to realize that it will be hard work to upgrade the culture and to exhibit a synthesis of the brain and heart. Individuals will need to develop confidence in their ability to coexist and collaborate and care about others who are not like themselves. The capacity to ask appropriate questions is an important factor in learning how to make new connections, how to collaborate and how to innovate continuously. Citizens will gain identity as a part of different networks of people with whom they are involved. Each person's identity in the future will come from a composite mosaic of connections with different people and different efforts both locally and in different parts of the world as they collaborate to create a vital and sustainable culture.

Elegance in Complexity

Elegance in complexity is a new concept that emphasizes the need to look for "access points" in order to help seed and evolve new capacities for a changing and dynamic society. In a search for access points of interest and learning potential, an upgrade of mental capacity is necessary to see emerging patterns in apparently chaotic situations requiring expanding knowledge. Developing transformational capacities will be required whether it is the capacity to use the Internet, the capacity to identify weak signals and know future trends, the capacity to think connectively or the capacity to become involved with electronic entrepreneurs throughout the world.

An Example: Principle 10

One afternoon an email message appeared on the computer screen of one of the COTF leaders. The message said that an entrepreneurial consultant of business change in England near Scotland's border had seen the Tartan Transformation Project website and was fascinated to know about the people who were involved with these types of ideas. A long distance email conversation began between North Carolina and England. The individual in England asked questions, offered suggestions and a reciprocal learning experience evolved. We asked him to be involved in a virtual learning conference initiated by the North Carolina Community College System. In each case, new knowledge was provided and we engaged in generational generative dialogue. This will become a major part of the COTF Second Enlightenment Project in order to help individuals involved not only learn knowledge about the First Enlightenment period, but to help them build bridges from the past to the future using the various techniques of Connective Thinking and Futures Generative Dialogue. In this way, we enhance culture by introducing new thinking capacities in fun and creative ways. As this new method is used in the Second Enlightenment Project, it will enhance the capacity of those involved in local communities to think differently and, through osmosis, feed continuous innovation into their culture.

Principle 11: Mix of Goodness and Skepticism, Integration of Reason and Mystery, Truth & Discovery Coexistent

Mix of Goodness and Skepticism

Francis Hutcheson and David Hume looked at humankind through two different prisms. Hutcheson saw and emphasized the potential for goodness in people. Hume was a skeptic who counseled safeguards to keep man in line with his passions.

Hutcheson observed that reason was the control for our passions. Hume focused on the fact that the passions should rule reason.The residual effect of this debate was to set up camps in which students of each reflected the emphasis of either one or the other factor as the determining factor in humankind's progress.

Integration of Reason and Mystery

The Enlightenment was a time when reason ruled. The reaction against myths and religion controlling our actions led to the consummate secular explorer and scientist. If it could not be experienced rationally, it was not true. Knowledge was fundamental as was proof. That which lurked in the crevices of man's mind as pure speculation without proof was to be discounted and discarded. We are, through reason, drifting back towards the speculative, we just call it "theoretical." The firm grip of Newton's laws of physics has shifted to the relativity of Einstein. The proven discoveries of Joseph Black, a preeminent chemist, were certain and sure. The early work of James Clerk Maxwell and later Stephen Hawkins often travels in lands that only the mystics can understand. And so we have come to a place in the journey where reason and mystery collide and one is as good as the other when each distinctive part of reality is visited. The future will reflect an integration of both ideas, as both the spiritual and physical find their respective places in the role of understanding reality.

Truth and Discovery Coexistent

We often mistake the search for truth for truth itself. When someone says, "I have the truth," it usually means, "I need certainty and have closed my mind to a different point of view." One of the great challenges of the future will be to have leaders at all levels who are not ideologues and who do not get caught up in the "truth of the moment." The Second Enlightenment will bring together different ways of looking at the world to help explain complexities. There will be little to no rearview truth related to increasing complexity. It will usually be in front of us. The capacity to discover will continue to impact what we understand truth to be. Our souls cannot be fed with materialism, but our schools and stomachs can. As we begin to develop the sophistication to see wholes and subtle nuances, we will understand how each of us can look at the same situation and see different truths. Our process of discovery allows us to see differences as appropriate and choose which difference we discover is true for us. Just as Einstein offered the concept of relativity to explain a physical truth of difference in perspective, so we will gain the maturity to understand relativity in how different people see the world and still maintain core values important to each of us. We will learn to build new truths from our own discoveries as we open our minds to new ideas. In so doing, we will not discard those existing beliefs that align with the future, but only add other ideas that we come to believe important.

An Example: Principle 11

There was once a chairman of a county public school board in 1980 whose concept of educational truth was focused on the one right way public education should be designed. To him, this meant a scope and sequence, with bits of knowledge offered in electives beyond a certain core curricula. It was the "truth" of how education should be accomplished. That same year he and another board member kept home schooling from being sanctioned by the board. Twenty years later, this same past chairman was asked (and accepted) to write a chapter in a book whose authors and editors were the leaders of the home schooling movement in the nation. Truth and discovery had come together for him over that twenty-year period because he had transformed his thinking about education and learning, and broadened his concept of what was truth. Learning to listen for the value in what others were saying, he connected the need for new ways of learning. He began to realize that the concept of truth is often multidimensional. There *is* more than one way to do things and he had to be open to discovery to see new truths. It is from this new stage of thinking that the concept of Transformational Learning emerged, a newly practical method of helping people learn how to make connections and develop innovative ideas within a changing context of the future.

Principle 12: Debate, Dialogue, Futures Generative Dialogue

Debate

Historically, the ability to present truth effectively was based on marshaling one's arguments in such a way that one's words overpowered another's point of view. The rise of debating societies honored this approach to finding truth within competing knowledge. It assumed that the winner had the truth and whoever was defeated did not. This was seen as a zero sum exercise. Increasingly, we realize that there can be value in what everyone says. Not that all of what one says will be on target, at times that is far from the truth. But debate divides the search for truth into dueling camps where one person looks for differences instead of the potential of what is said. In this age of interconnections, we need to find ways for humans to connect and search for new truths together.

Dialogue

David Bohm was a particle physicist who looked at the subatomic level of life. As he explored the forces that kept physical reality together, he began to experience the sense that there were common forces in social reality that were as important as muons and tychions. This realization started his search for common human forces in society and led him to the discovery that dialogue performs the same function in society as does weak forces at the subatomic level. It was in dialogue that he found human forces that brought people together. It was debate that forced them apart. He began to develop initial conditions for a study and enhancement of dialogue leading him to the conclusion that much of leadership in the future would be providing the capacities to build an environment that diverse people would seek as a safe haven to offer their opinions and suggestions. Unless one had something to add to what had been said, silence was appropriate. Bohm found that the use of body language, appropriate questions and indirect techniques were equal in importance to that of the physical forces he had spent his whole life studying. The physicist spent the last years of his life exploring the connective forces of human dialogue.

Futures Generative Dialogue

COTF has developed an extension of the concept of dialogue. It is called Futures Generative Dialogue. By developing dialogue within the context of future trends and emerging "weak signals," newly innovative and transformative ideas will emerge that are not about old ideas. In a connective, and/both dialogue, existing knowledge and knowledge of emerging weak signals combine to create generative ideas. Any good leader of Futures Generative Dialogue will know how to introduce information about future trends that are not a part of the conversation.

Good strategies are:

1) to quote other people that are experts in their fields,
2) refer to other articles and
3) bring attention to websites full of futures thinking.

A futures generative dialogue requires an understanding of how to make connections and how to challenge existing assumptions.

An Example: Principle 12

At a meeting of 40 people in Europe who were outstanding thinkers, brought together to talk about key issues, ground rules were provided for dialogue. If anyone was to talk, the person had to have something to add to what was previously said, otherwise keep quiet. When someone talked, make sure it was connected and not a departure from the subject at hand. As the dialogue evolved there were times when silence was the rule. However, the conclusions that the group reached, through silence and dialogue were far better than those they could have reached through debate. Another group in the United States brought individuals together at a local level to have a Futures Generative Dialogue to talk about how to rethink the way a rural leadership development institute could be repositioned at the cutting edge. The use of Futures Generative Dialogue introduced new concepts of leadership that led to a new concept, a parallel approach where traditional leadership concepts and techniques are used for short-term projects and Master Capacity Builder leadership concepts and techniques are used to help local groups understand how to talk about long-term issues within a futures context.

Principle 13: One Best Answer, Choices, The Concept Of Applied Appropriateness

One Best Answer

Over the last twenty years, the concepts of strategic planning and standardized educational practices have intersected to reinforce the idea of looking for the one best answer. The idea of a standard model assumes that there is one approach, one best answer, which will be appropriate for all situations. This is a first cousin idea to the Scottish Enlightenment concept that diverse people would react the same if found in the same situation. While this idea might have some truth in a time of stability, we increasingly live in a time of history when individuals are required to adapt to constantly changing circumstances, *according to the expectations of those involved.* There may be one best answer for a particular person in a particular situation, however, there are many choices emerging in this time of constant change, especially when diverse human beings face the challenges of community transformation.

Choices

We live in an age of choices. Nowhere is this better evidenced than going to the grocery store. In 1950 there were, on the average, 900 different items in a grocery store. In 2016, the larger super markets have 80,000 items. The average number in an average store is 42,000. There are choices of entertainment and choices of cell phones. We are inundated with choices. *One of the most important ideas emerging from new thinking is that the use of self-organizing systems will let communities adapt to changing conditions if they prepare and anticipate what may occur in the future.* Scenario planning was developed to help organizations plan for a future full of choices, yet with no certainty of which scenario would occur. As choices are made, the prepared organization/ community will have a built-in feedback system or systems to give an understanding of the results of the actions taken. Until a community develops capacities for transformation which allow multiple choices, and provides new avenues for community research and design, the focus will continue to be on developing the one best answer, a certain prescription for frustration.

The Concept of Applied Appropriateness

Of all the questions that will become central to the leadership of any local community, the one most valuable will be "what is appropriate in this situation?" This type of question will provide a flexibility and adaptability of thinking which will minimize turf wars and neutralize most efforts to control dialogue or the decision making processes. With this question, the door opens to identify trends of the future and to build a context within which to consider any issue or to generate new ideas not existing in the past. Open-ended questions allow for the one best standard answer when it is appropriate and, also, to search for multiple choices when needed. Each group entertaining this question will need to understand the framework and scope of the situation. Is there a short- or long-term need? What types of issues are involved? What changes are expected in the next ten years that will impact this situation? What are all the factors that need to be considered? Once these are determined, a context emerges, and a process can be designed that will provide a set of smaller parallel processes with which to move forward. Until the concept of Applied Appropriateness becomes a tool in the toolbox of community transformation, there will continue to be debate, conflict, frustration, turf wars and out of date choices.

An Example: Principle 13

Select any profession. If the concept of "best practices" applies to the situation, then use best practices. If there is a need to rethink existing practices, then use Futures Generative Dialogue for research and development. If there is a need to focus on the short term, use strategic planning. If the need is long term, apply the idea of adaptive planning. In all cases, remember, no matter what is decided, there is another set of ideas and actions that will be just as appropriate if you apply them differently or have different expectations. The future is an "and/both" world and, as a leader, you will need to think at different levels, in different ways, at different times. This "matrix thinking" will open your mind and create new ideas at the same time that you consider what to do.

Principle 14: Representative Democracy, Electronic Republic, Polycentric Democracy/Mobile Collaborative Governance

Representative Democracy

The concept of representative democracy is the gift of the constitutional convention in 1787 and reflects the structure of a republic. Many people say that we don't have a democracy, we have a republic. We have both. We have a democracy (Greek for sovereignty of the people) and a republic. It is not a direct democracy, where all citizens vote on every issue. The concept of popular sovereignty insured that ultimate power resides in the people. As the society has become more complex, money oriented and media driven, power has shifted to the representatives. It is the challenge of our existing democracy to rethink how we need to be organized and what decision making processes will be appropriate for a more complex society where the Internet will connect people of all locations and points of view.

Electronic Republic

Lawrence Grossman, author of the book, *Electronic Republic*, charts the history of the idea of democracy and predicts that increasingly, we will use electronic infrastructure as our tool for making democracy work in an era of complex issues, multiple choices and transforming communities. We are in a transition in which we will work with hybrid systems of decision making and technologies to see what will work and what will be inappropriate. Washington, DC among other cities has used elements of electronic democracy to add transparency and trust in the creation of budgets and issue priorities. We predict that the role of the elected official will shift to more of a facilitator of new thinking and transformational capacity building in order to insure that all levels of our society will broaden the involvement of interested citizens. One of the most important concerns of an Electronic Republic is to understand that the processes designed must align with the emerging structure of the society. To this end, Second Enlightenment ideas have been conceived to undergird a philosophy that is consistent with a diverse, technically driven democratic population.

Polycentric Democracy/Mobile Collaborative Governance

The future vitality of our democracy requires a hybrid of direct and representative methods. Local citizens need to regain a sense of control over local decision making, as there is more and more change in communities. Many people have expressed that they lack the ability to impact issues important to their lives. In the future, elected representatives will maintain decision making responsibilities at the same time that they find themselves the facilitators of new types of citizen processes. This varies from the excellent work of Democracy in Action (short-term decision making for existing community issues) to the Mobile Collaborative Governance process being pioneered by the Center for Communities of the Future. The Mobile Collaborative Governance process is a part of the overall concept of Polycentric Democracy, and is based on the concept that people want to be involved with community issues that are the most important to them, and have control over the decision making process.

The Mobile Collaborative Governance process is designed to involve citizens in different ways at different levels. The most innovative of these ideas is a four-phase process to have citizens in control of each phase:

1) identify key issues of concern to the community,
2) hold a Citizens Congress to identify key factors of the most important issue identified (within a futures context),
3) have Direct Consensus Democracy teams work to develop

strategies to resolve the issue, and

4) have all interested citizens vote to select the most appropriate strategy (manually or electronically).

One last word on the Rise of a Second Enlightenment

The very ideas that emerged from the Scottish minds and pens of Patrick Geddes, Adam Smith, Adam Ferguson, Dugald Stewart, David Hume, Lord Kames and many others, are the ideas that have held our society together for two hundred years. If these same men returned to this time in history, they would wonder why so many leaders are being conservative in a time of radical change. You can just hear David Hume, one of the fathers of the concept of individual rights, huff in exasperation, "don't these people know that we were considered radicals because of the magnitude of change we proposed? If anything, you need to think as we thought. You need to offer ideas that history will later be seen as a Second Enlightenment."

It *is* time for a new framework of ideas to undergird the emerging society. A society in constant change that will be increasingly interconnected, independent and complex. We offer these concepts as a starting point for Futures Generative Dialogue leading to connections with interested people and organizations in other states and countries. There is no more important effort for academia, working in collaboration with local communities, than to build capacities for transformation in the thinking of leaders of our society. Einstein once said, "We stand on the shoulders of giants." It is to the giants of the First Enlightenment that this concept to evolve interlocking networks and organizations to think about a Second Enlightenment is dedicated. May we show the same noble commitment to develop an intellectual philosophy as appropriate to today as was classical liberalism to the time of these magnificent Scots whose ideas reached around the world.

Chapter 2

Master Capacity Builders for Community Transformation

The concept of leadership in the 21st Century needs to be consistent with the type of society that is emerging. The most significant changes in leadership reflect the transformations that are occurring in the society – a society that is evolving from a structure of hierarchies, standard answers and predictability, to one that is based on interlocking networks, multiple outcomes, and a comfort with ambiguity and uncertainty. Of most importance, society will be constantly changing, interactive, interdependent and increasingly complex.

A key challenge in today's world of constant change is to realize that traditional leadership concepts and methods, while appropriate for current projects that have defined outcomes, are often counter-productive for the kind of transformational capacity building that will be necessary for the future vitality of communities. 21st century leadership will require more than just shifting from tasks to processes, or from linear thinking to systemic thinking. It will require rethinking the very nature of the overall leadership experience.

The concept of 21st century community transformation recognizes that there will be times when traditional leadership ideas are appropriate and times when new leadership ideas will need to be used.

The following chart compares attributes of traditional leadership and transformative leadership. Each person and group will need to develop the judgment to choose which needs to be emphasized based on each situation and the overall long-term goal of the organization and community:

	Traditional Builder	Master Capacity Builder
Short-term situation	Takes immediate action	Considers the long-term effect
Long-term issue	Predicts a specific outcome with predetermined accountability	Anticipates what may emerge using trends and weak signals
Concept of Planning	Strategic planning and linear	Adaptive planning and non-linear
Concept of standards	Focuses on Structure	Emphasizes alternatives, feedback and networks
Concept of Thinking	Focuses on absolute answers and singular truths	Emphasizes being open to new ideas and choices
Focus	Concerned for how action impacts the leader	Concern for how action impacts the situation and others
Use of Brain	Emphasizes left brain	Emphasizes integration of right and left brain

Emotional Attributes	Emphasizes action, being right, strong opinions	Emphasizes patience, caring, openness to new ideas
Ethics	Concern for "the" truth	Concern for truth(s)
Concept of the individual	Independent and self-sufficient	Inter-dependent and self-reliant
Concept of others	Compares to one's existing beliefs	Embraces diversity and openness of thinking

The 21st Century ushers in a dynamic future and an emergent structure. There are no models to use. There are few past experiences that will help us to know how to lead in a constantly changing, interconnected, interdependent and increasingly complex society.

Peter Drucker, noted futurist and management scholar, suggests that:

> *Every few hundred years in Western history there occurs a sharp transformation. Within a few short decades, society – its world view, its basic values, its social and political structures, its arts, its key institutions – rearranges itself ... We are currently living through such a time.*

Too many of the trends we now see gathering speed suggest that traditional ideas and systems are quite unsustainable. For example:

- Declining trust in government and other sources of traditional authority and lack of confidence in 'legacy institutions'.
- Increasing consumption of non-renewable resources to the extent that it would now take four planet earths to meet the needs of the world's population if we all live the U.S. lifestyle.
- Rapidly growing inequality, within and between countries, and among demographic groups on almost any measure – education, wealth, life expectancy, access to opportunity.
- Increased levels of stress-related and other mental illness, self-harm, violence and personal disorientation in society.
- Increased volatility in a number of systems – stock markets, trade, the weather system, commodity markets, etc.

As a result, we need a new concept of leadership to complement the traditional leadership practices of strategic planning, outcomes based analysis, and top down command and control leadership in order to be able to build capacities for transformation that will provide individuals, organizations and communities the ability to adapt quickly to changing conditions.

Master Capacity Builders Provide Leadership in the Context of Historical Transition

What theory of leadership is appropriate in a context that is changing in kind as well as scope? Does experience always help, or is experience at times an obstacle? Are new principles of leadership applied the same in both public and private sectors? What will be the attributes of leadership in the 21st century?

The model of 21st century Comprehensive Community Transformation recognizes that there will be times when traditional leadership ideas are appropriate and times when an emerging, new type of leadership will be needed. This new leadership is called Transformational Leadership and the practitioners are Master Capacity Builders. Traditional leadership if focused on objectives and outcomes. A Master Capacity Builder is focused on identifying emerging weak signals connecting innovative ideas and collaborative people, and building capacities for transformation through the design of parallel processes as a part of community research and development.

Traditional leadership emphasizes the use of projects and is measured by concrete outcomes. Transformational Leadership emphasizes the use of building webs of relationships, creating interlocking networks, and innovation ecosystems. It is these skills that will develop the ability of people, organizations and communities to be able to adapt quickly to constantly changing conditions and situations.

If the need is to help people think differently, be open to new ideas, test new innovative concepts, link diverse people in collaboration, and consider issues within a futures context, then new transformational leadership approaches of a Master Capacity Builder are needed. The emphasis needs to shift from immediate actions to generative dialogue that leads to specific transformational ideas. The strategic planning principles of prediction and control will shift to adaptive planning principles of self-organization and emergence.

Holistic thinking and adaptive planning are replacing strategic planning. Processes that connect diverse people and ideas in generative innovation become as important as specific plans and expected outcomes. A Master Capacity Builder is always focused on transformational ideas and methods.

It is very difficult for people to embrace change of any type. Years of standard outcomes and cherished beliefs insure that the majority of people will resist change. Transformational Leaders need to understand that transformation of ideas and actions will take time and cannot be forced. Great patience will be needed by

Master Capacity Builders to create an environment where people come to their own conclusions about the need for change. Transformational Leaders should never take negative direct comments, body language or reactions personally.

There will be many situations when these new leaders will need to introduce innovative ideas or create times of tension which are necessary to establish an environment to sow seeds of transformation. In those times, irritations and discomfort will be evident, and usually those affected will not be willing to express their reactions because they are threatened by what is being said or what is occurring.

A true Transformational Leader and Master Capacity Builder understands the need for growth within individuals and among groups. This leader cares more about helping the person, organization and community leaders grow in understanding than he or she cares about being liked. The traditional leader is focused on outcomes and results at all times no matter what the cost to the spirit of those involved. For Master Capacity Builders, the true concern is exactly as the name suggests – to develop transformational capacities for all involved.

A Master Capacity Builder understands that for transformational learning experiences to occur, personal growth (to include becoming open to new ideas without being threatened) can be more important than outcomes if the objective is to create an environment and culture for transformation, whether in an organization or the community.

If the objective of leadership is the success of short-term projects and meeting preset standards, then traditional concepts are appropriate. If the objective of leadership is to evolve a climate and culture conducive to real transformation of thinking, attitudes and behavior, then emphasis needs to shift to how to connect diverse people and how to introduce weak signals, emerging trends and transformational concepts into the thinking and activities of the organization or community.

The development of the concept of Master Capacity Builder is divided into four parts:

I   Understanding the Context
II   Seeing the Need
III   Developing the Knowledge and Skills
IV   Building Capacities for Transformation

Understanding the Context

US companies are expected to ship more than 200,000 service jobs to countries like India every year.
The New Face of the Silicon Age, Wired Magazine, February 2004

The definition of illiteracy in the 21st century will be the inability to learn, unlearn, and relearn.
Alvin Toffler

Sensor nets will let us relieve the human being of the responsibility of drawing information out of the physical world.
David Tennenhouse, Defense Advanced Research Project Agency

Ours is a magnificently creative era. But that creativity produces change, and that change attracts enemies, philosophical as well as self-interested.
Virginia Postrel, The Future and Its Enemies

The great challenge of our time is to build and nurture sustainable communities—social, cultural and physical environments in which we can satisfy our needs and aspirations without diminishing the chances of future generations.
Fritjof Capra, The Turning Point

We usually offer one or two quotes to lead into a new idea. Here five are introduced to reflect the importance of understanding the context of our times, a time of historical transition from a society organized around principles of physics (Industrial Age) to one based on biology and ecology (Ecological Civilization). No one or two quotes can provide a true sense of the nature of the ongoing change in our society. Even five quotes, which focus on different aspects of our time of transformation, cannot do justice to the systemic, complex change which threatens to overwhelm our capacity to understand and evolve in effective ways as a new society emerges. It is this need to understand the transforming context of our society and world that is the basis for the concept of Master Capacity Builder.

In 1983 Fritjof Capra wrote a book called *Turning Point*, a book whose basic premise was "that an emerging paradigm is replacing – or at least competing with – the view of the universe that has guided our civilization since the days of Sir Isaac Newton and Rene Descartes." Some considered the word "paradigm" nothing but jargon. Bob Theobald (*The Rapids of Change*) helped us understand that what was occurring around us was nothing less than transformational requiring a new context and new language.

What I think has happened in the last thirty years is that we've been building towards change. The change process appears to happen slowly, but of course it doesn't. You have to do the building, and then some catalytic process comes along and people say, "Oh! Everything has changed." But the everything changing does not happen overnight. It happens because of all the previous work. I think we're at the point where massive positive change can happen. That's where it's different today.
Bob Theobald

In retrospect, change was occurring faster than we realized. By 1980, many traditional industries were being relocated overseas as a result of the growing interactive global economy. In May 1981, the prime rate of interest was 20%. By 1987 the Iran-Contra scandal had brought dishonor to a political arena still scarred by Watergate. For the first time, we were beginning to question what is wrong. The *Turning Point* posited that all these factors were not as independent and separate as they seemed on the surface. They were, in fact, connected in many different and subtle ways. Unless one could see relationships, creative connections and think systemically, one would not be able to understand the emerging future that would be very different from the past, nor be able to function effectively within an increasingly fast-paced and complex society.

In the 35 years since the *Turning Point* was published, we have begun to see the world as interconnected. We are convinced that we are living in a time of such historical transformation that the very context of our lives is transforming. And unless we rethink all aspects of our lives, communities and societies, we will find ourselves increasingly agitated, frustrated and giving into the fear of being out of control.

Unless we adapt and become able to see new patterns and recognize new rules our society and economy is in danger of imploding. In addition, there is the wild card, the idea of conscious evolution. The concept that mankind has developed enough knowledge about how nature works that we are able to impact how our species evolves. The advances in communication technologies, brain research, genetic engineering, and nanotechnology will allow materials, human enhancement and biodiversity to be designed and created that nature has not provided.

It is this challenging change, in context of our society that explains why Master Capacity Builders are needed. We believe this is so important that 60% of our time is spent working with the concept of Transformational Learning, developing local leaders as Master Capacity Builders, and connecting colleagues who should know each other. Until local leaders and citizens begin to think differently, and until new capacities for transformation are introduced into the thinking and activities of local communities, we will not have vital and sustainable economies and societies. Since there are few local leaders familiar with the ideas and methods of community transformation, there is an immediate need to create Master Capacity Builders who can help build these 21st century capacities in local areas.

A first step in introducing those interested in becoming Master Capacity Builders is to make sure they become familiar with what we mean by the phrase "transforming the context."

This T-Bar Table of Transformation identifies a number of the key categories of transformation. Subsequent sections of this chapter will discuss these ideas and strategies, what capacity building processes are important, what leadership techniques need to be used and in what ways a Master Capacity Builder can coach local leaders as agents of transformation.

Industrial Society	Ecological Civilization
Fossil Fuels	Green Energy and Hydrogen
Mechanical Macro Technology	Electronic, Micro and Nano Technology
Economic Development by Recruiting Industrial Jobs	Economic Development by comprehensive Community Transformation
Health – Cure Existing Problems by Surgery and Drugs	Health – Prevent Existing Problems by Biotechnology Alternative Medicine

Education Focusing on Past Knowledge	Learning Focusing on Future Trends Connecting Disparate Ideas Leading to Continuous Innovation
Innovation Focused on Things	Innovation focused on Ideas, Creativity and Imagination
Linear Either/Or Thinking	Non-linear, And/Both Thinking
Strategic Planning	Adaptive Planning
Representative Democracy	Hybrid of Representative and Polycentric Democracy
Task Orientated Outcomes	Transformative, Capacity Building
Nation State Focused	Global and City State Focused
White, Male Authority	Gender, Ethnic Equity
Emphasis of Human Domain	Human, Ecological Balance

Seeing the Need

Until now, ours has been a dance with the ordinary.
Thomas Frey

Any individual who aspires to become a Master Capacity Builder needs to understand that there are new principles of community transformation that need to be understood and applied. It also helps to understand that no one changes unless the need to change is seen, understood, and accepted.

The role of a Master Capacity Builder is to help local leaders understand:

1) How to identify and analyze an emerging situation as different from the past,
2) How to create an environment where citizens see the need to transform their view of the world, and
3) How to identify access points that allow a Master Capacity Builder to seed transformational thinking and action that helps individuals and groups begin to rethink their resistance to change and to understand the difference between reforming change and transforming change.

Master Capacity Builders need to be able to differentiate between two types of change:

- Reforming change – the type of change that enhances or refines what has been done traditionally and either increases or decreases the degree of what has occurred for years.

- Transforming change – this type of change challenges the very nature and underlying assumption of what has been done.

Reforming change is usually focused on short-term needs and transforming change emphasizes a longer-term perspective that requires the following attributes of Master Capacity Builders.

Patience, ability to anticipate responses, ability to read body language

Remember that an individual needs to understand why change is necessary and appropriate. A Master Capacity Builder can use articles and websites, or cite TV shows and poems, quotes or other examples to introduce new ideas. In addition, one needs to learn how to ask questions that create a positive tension where an individual is challenged at multiple levels. Tell a story in one's own life illustrating the particular issue of transformation that has been introduced. The Master Capacity Builder can invite other folks to share thoughts and as they do, their thoughts can be validated and connected to the thoughts of other people as well.

Always remember that a Master Capacity Builder needs to show in his or her own leadership style the need to change, without overdoing it.

This is most effectively done by giving testimonials and stories about ways in which you decided you needed to change:

1)   when the situation happened
2)   when you realized you needed to change
3)   why it was important for you to change and
4)   a specific example how the change has impacted your ability to be a better Transformational Leader as a result of one's own personal transformation

Openness to new ideas and ability to see transformational potential

Introduce a personal story as illustrated above or tell a story of someone else that illustrates an example of becoming open to new ideas. One can also ask others to go to specific websites; give them a question that brings an idea of a need for personal transformation to their radar screen indirectly. Ask them to see if there are any stories or examples that they think illustrate a way in which they need to change to be a Master Capacity Builder.

Introduce an area of community life and ask those with whom you are working to identify weak signals and trends and determine how these emerging new ideas or factors will impact their community, their organizations, and themselves. Ask them what will need to be transformed to be able to adapt to these impacts.

Passion for learning and ability to see connections:

Give folks a list of a) 10 articles, b) 10 websites, and c) 10 books.

Have them select a category of community life. Don't tell them what to do. Tell them it's up to them to determine what to read. Ask the question, "What will you need to do to prepare your organization and community for the impact of the future trends you have selected?" When they return for a futures generative dialogue with their selections in hand, have another question ready to use such as, "As a result of your analysis of the impacts of the weak signals or trends you selected, is there one or more ways you need to change to be able to be a transformational leader with regard to the particular issue?"

One of the greatest challenges in an effort to create an environment for personal, organizational and community trans-formation is to help people learn to be "and/both," and not "either/or" thinkers. Our culture and educational system is based on a set of fundamental ideas which include the objectives that: 1) there is one best answer, 2) personal independence is sacred, and 3) the market will provide the one price that maximizes profit.

We even phrase our questions to force one answer (e.g. "Is the reason that the team didn't win the fault of the coach or the fact that the best player was sick?" Probably neither, if the team was beaten by 35 points). There is usually more than one factor or answer that is involved, especially if the situation or issue is complex. Therefore, for someone to see the need to change, he or she often needs to learn how to be an "and/both" thinker to be able to see that there may be more than one way to look at an existing issue or emerging need. Also, unless a person becomes an "and/both" thinker, he or she will not be able to listen to see value in what someone else says and, therefore, to connect an idea to other ideas which is the mechanism of innovation. This is the skill of a "connective listener" who is able to connect with others in deep, creative collaboration. One of the most important transformations that will occur in the 21st century is a shift from radical individualism to a new concept called "connected individuality."

A different kind of listening; the ability to look for multiple answers; the ability to learn how to be a matrix thinker.

A Master Capacity Builder is responsible for helping people see connections that are not readily apparent using traditional linear thinking. Non-linear, connective, and/both thinking is difficult to develop due to the way those in Western Culture have been educated. As a result, a Master Capacity Builder needs to use multiple methods to help local leaders come to realize that, in many cases, there are multiple approaches, solutions and innovative ideas that are appropriate. One of the most effective approaches to creating an environment where a shift in thinking will occur is to design a system of transformational thinking using two or more of the following techniques:

- One on one dialogue introducing new factors which will cause new ways of understanding beyond "one factor thinking."
- Play a game that introduces new trends in a way where multiple possibilities may be correct.
- Tell a story about the shift in thinking that led you or

someone else to an "and/both" approach.

- Use questions which will require the "linear thinker" to broaden his/her perspective (e.g. "what are all the factors that need to be considered?").
- Have individuals work with "bubble diagrams" to develop "big ideas" where there is no one answer, and where a system of ideas needs to be connected for a more complex idea of transformation to emerge.
- Point out when someone asks you an either/or question that you think both answers are correct and appropriate, and explain why.

In most cases, local leaders have deep roots of experience and traditional thinking that is the basis for their success. One of the well-known principles of change is that change usually occurs only when old ways are no longer seen to work or when there is a crisis. What increases the difficulty of seeing the need for change in a time of transformation is that one cannot predict what will happen, and new methods and tools do not exist that will be needed to deal with situations and issues never before encountered.

Understand how to search for weak signals; ability to introduce ideas indirectly.

Read newspapers from *USA Today* and the *Wall Street Journal* to the *New York Times* or magazines such as *The Futurist, Wired, Fast Company* and *MIT Technology Journal* and identify websites for compelling events, episodes or new situations.

There are four stages of transformation and all the phases require constant analysis, understanding, leadership, risk and continuous evolution of new capacities.

The four stages of transformation are:

1) Resistance to change
2) The "hmmm" period
3) A time of "ahas" and
4) "Off course, it is"

Seeing the need to change comes during the third, or "aha!" phase. This is the most important of the four phases because once a person begins to think about and question one's traditional ideas, he or she will provide a sign in some way that an opening to new thinking is possible. The experienced Master Capacity Builder will continuously look for some sign that the person is ready to see the need for change, and be ready to act in an appropriate way. It is important to realize that once someone enters the "hmmm zone" you've got them and they will never go back. Help "nudge" the individual, yet let any individual evolve in his or her own way. Do not be afraid to let folks tussle a bit within themselves since there cannot be deep growth and personal transformation without early resistance and struggle.

Developing Knowledge and Skills to Be a Master Capacity Builder

To lead people, walk behind them.
Lao Tzu

A Master Capacity Builder is not created overnight. No one seminar or short training course will develop these capacities in someone who decides he or she wants to become an effective Transformational Leader.

The leader that is focused on helping others develop long-term capacities for transformation will need to become a specialized generalist, a 21st century Renaissance Thinker. An irony of our age is that as knowledge explodes with the result of the creation of micro-specialists, there is an increasing need for the development of a new type of person skilled in an updated (uplearn) concept of liberal arts. All effective leaders of a new kind of social, political and economic innovation (transformation) will need to have broad and deep knowledge in many areas in order to:

- To be able to see new connections and patterns that others cannot see.
- To be able to ask questions that are appropriate and that help others:
  - See the need to transform
  - Become open to new ideas
  - Introduce a new idea into a generative dialogue
  - Develop and shift ownership of new innovations and concepts
- To insure that insecure people cannot control, dominate or derail any transformative process.
- To create innovative frameworks for:
  - Projects
  - Generative dialogue and
  - Parallel processes
- To be able to facilitate futures generative dialogue processes among diverse people of all kinds.
- To help people of all backgrounds be able to understand and utilize ideas and mechanisms at a higher level of complexity.

Building Capacities for Transformation.

Courage is what it takes to stand up and speak. Courage is also what it takes to sit down and listen.
Winston Churchill

Building Parallel Processes

One of the most important mechanisms of community transformation is the ability to understand how to design and utilize parallel processes. Within our system of transformation there is the need for parallel ideas, actions, connections, capacities and decisions to be created and made simultaneously. This cannot be done with the use of linear thinking and singular, linear processes. Therefore, our Master Capacity Builders must become a "master" (thus the use of the term) in how to organize and facilitate multiple efforts, projects, and processes in parallel that will move at different rates, in different directions and with different consequences. Since there is no one answer or no one factor that is controlling in community transformation, a Master Capacity Builder will be required to balance multiple balls and processes simultaneously with other people connected into a "team of transformative facilitators". The following identifies different types of parallel processes:

- Short term and longer term.
- Action (outcomes) and capacity building (transformation).
- Creating multiple nodes and evolving into a connective network/web.
- Meeting the multiple needs of a system in transformation.
- Develop theory, concepts, methods and techniques simultaneously.
- Futures Generative Dialogue and spin-off projects evolving in mutual interaction.

Small Group Facilitation

One of the core capacity building methods is small group facilitation. This methodology allows a Master Capacity Builder to frame what happens without the need for control. The following outlines diverse types of small groups with key objectives, considerations and facilitation techniques:

Capacity Building Seminar: The objectives of a transformative capacity building seminar are to:

- Introduce those attending to the concept of community transformation.
- Identify whether transformative capacities and skills are important for the topic at hand.
- Show how it connects to the overall system of community transformation.
- Provide examples and hands-on exercises to show how specific capacities/skills are introduced and developed.

Ask an Appropriate Question

There are many different types of questions that become important to any system of community transformation. Two objectives are key:

1 To introduce the participants to a family of different types of questions and how they can be used
2 To develop the actual skill of being able to design, time and ask appropriate questions

Futures Generative Dialogue

The objective of a Futures Generative Dialogue is twofold:

a) To understand how a dialogue is different from a discussion
b) To help participants identify weak signals and trends, consider their potential impact and learn how a futures context is designed

Futures Project Development

A key method of building capacities for transformation is to design "futures processes" that introduce new, innovative ideas in a practical way into the thinking and activities of a community. There are many types of processes.

Each Futures Process has three stages of development:

- The idea is created as a spin-off of a Futures Generative Dialogue.
- An adaptive plan developed with parallel processes designed to involve multiple people for multiple reasons.
- Implementation of the project is begun with looking for access points and seeding futures thinking and capacities for transformation.

The concept of building capacities for transformation has emerged from the research and development work of the Center for Communities of the Future over the last twenty years. It takes time for "transformational seeds" to be planted and grow over months and years because the concepts, methods, techniques and skills for building capacities for transformation are significantly different compared to traditional leadership approaches and short-term decision making. Whereas short-term projects use direct action, benchmarking and standard model evaluation methods, long-term transformative capacity building relies on identifying weak signals, looking for access points to seed new ways of thinking and designing systems of parallel processes. *Therefore, all methods of building capacities for transformation are based on research and development.*

The idea of a Master Capacity Builder has emerged in the thinking of leadership development as a result of the increased volatility and ambiguity inherent in the transition of society from an Industrial Age to an Ecological Civilization. A traditional leader experienced in strategic planning that has predefined outcomes and standard measurements is unprepared for a society that is constantly changing and that requires the new concept of "adaptive planning." It will be imperative for local communities to develop pools of "master capacity builders" able to adapt and help others learn how to adapt to changing conditions as our society becomes more interdependent, interconnected, fast-paced, and increasingly complex.

In the next section of the book we will take a look at four key sectors undergoing vast change and how transformational processes are at work in accelerating efficiencies and better outcomes. The four sectors include higher education, the emerging molecular economy, government and citizen engagement and finally, health and wellness. There is a call to action in each of these sectors for leaders and citizens from all walks of life to become engaged. Each person has a voice in how decisions are made affecting the lives of our children, neighbors and ourselves.

Chapter 3

Transformational Learning: The Foundation for Future Forward Colleges & Continuous Uplearning

Transformational Learning

Higher Education is in a state of flux. We are entering a new historical period in which machines (advanced computers, robotics and genomic technology) are overtaking jobs traditionally done by humans. Our society is transforming from hierarchies, standard answers, and predictability to interlocking networks and ecosystems, multiple answers and the need to be comfortable with ambiguity and uncertainty. As a result, all aspects of the traditional learning experience are under stress and will morph into new patterns and approaches as our interdependent world challenges past truths of leadership, economic development, governance, and education – especially education and learning – as the need for resilience and the capacity to adapt quickly become central to the vitality, sustainability and success of any community and nation.

We teach today, with only slight variations, in ways that have been consistent for the past several hundred years. We typically teach ideas and methods that have been developed for past situations, without regard to futures thinking because change occurred relatively slowly until recently. *As a result, we are past-acclimated, not future focused.* In this emerging age of constant change, we need to be future focused. Students and their parents are demanding changes that provide for more accountability, better outcomes and lower tuition.

Future Forward Colleges (term coined at Wake Tech Community College in Raleigh, NC) will need to be radically different – transformed – from current models. Rapid technological change, the need for more rapid response, and increased human-interconnectedness will continue to drive innovation and change across the world into the future.

Instead of long periods of certainty, there will be much uncertainty and volatility. Traditional models cannot adapt quickly enough to meet the needs of an emerging future that will constantly change. There will be a need to re-conceptualize all institutions through processes of creative collaboration. There will be a need for collaborative risk takers to co-create transformative ideas and methods and test new approaches to the future.

As we shift from an Industrial Age to an Ecological Civilization that will require quick adaptation to constant change, our society becomes more fast-paced and interconnected. Rapid technological change is driving innovation, leading to new processes and interconnected webs of new information, deeper collaboration and emerging knowledge. Technological change requires post-secondary education's role to be transformed in preparing an educated society and a competent workforce. Students need to "unlearn" traditional concepts and methods as the only means of learning and "uplearn" ideas and methods to enhance their capacity to understand and work. The concept of uplearning is defined as the ability to think at a higher level of connections and complexity. This requires not just a change on the part of the student (who is very likely to be adaptive to new ideas and methods), but requires a change on the part of educators, who were schooled in traditional ways of educating youth and adults. There is a call to action for both educators who must adapt their pedagogy and for students who must embrace continuous, transformational learning.

Traditional education in Western Culture is based on two assumptions, rationality and knowledge that already exists ... and by defin-

ition, looks backward for guidance. In an age of exponential change,
the skills of intuition, insight, imagination and innovation are key
to success, and, by definition looks forward for guidance.
Richard Ogle Smart World

If the direction of learning needs to shift from looking backwards to looking to the future, it is important to understand how the context of society is transforming. In understanding this unseen phenomenon of societal transformation, educators are able to determine the best learning environments and practices to prepare students with essential skills in a time of constant change. The context of emerging knowledge becomes equally as important as the content of existing knowledge.

Existing educational approaches need to be systemically transformed to develop learners with the knowledge and skills required for a society and economy whose patterns are just beginning to be identified. Colleges (especially community colleges) and universities should rethink their roles, structure, and learning methodology to be able to create an environment for learning that supports transformational thinking and action. As educational costs continue to rise, and the demand for lifelong learning and uplearning increases as exponential change occurs, the proximity of community colleges within local areas will insure that large numbers of citizens are given the capacities to adapt to new ideas and approaches of a society and economy in complete transformation.

With this in mind, the following attempts to identify key changes in learning systems that will be needed during this time of historical transition that will significantly impact the development of learners able to navigate an adaptive societal and economic environment:

- A shift from teaching singular, standard answers to teaching emerging connections leading to innovation and new ideas

- A shift from the exclusive use of individual learning around standard answers to individualized learning utilizing teams and networks.
- A shift from teaching linear thinking to teaching non-linear systems and connective thinking.
- A shift from educational leadership by individual instructors to leadership by teams and adaptive learning networks.
- A shift from organization of command and control to organization by interlocking networks and self-organizing "units," breaking down silos and operational overlap within the college.
- A shift from instructional methods of one-way content delivery (the "sage on the stage") to real-time interactive learning.
- A shift from reliance on historically-based knowledge to emerging knowledge connecting disparate "idea spaces."
- A shift to content delivery through mobile technologies that will provide distributive knowledge and individu-alized learning at any time from any place.

These new learning and instructional norms reflect the need for all learning organizations to adapt to the ongoing transforma-tions in society to include:

- A shift from independence as the central organizing principle of society to interdependence as the norm as we deal with increasing connectedness and complexity.
- A shift from radical individuality to connected individu-ality.
- A shift from hyper-competition to deeper collaboration to be able to adapt quickly to changing circumstances.
- A shift from an economy and society based on principles

of physics (linear, cause and effect and strategic planning) to an economy and society based on biological principles and interlocking networks able to adapt to constant change.

- A shift from workforce development based on technology and computer skills only to a Future Forward Workforce based on creativity, connective thinking, innovation networks and ability to identify weak signals.

Lifelong learning of all kinds in the future will need forward-thinking people to join in collaboration to be actively engaged in a new evolution of teaching (facilitating as guides of learning). People will be needed who care about all forms of learning, and who also understand that what we are doing in higher education is not working for a new society and economy whose patterns are just starting to form. These will be the educators of the future. We will need leaders and faculty who are able to connect disparate ideas, people and processes in order to rethink and redesign higher education for a "world that is still coming into existence."

During the evolution of all disruptive and transformational efforts throughout history, there have been those who fight it, and those who embrace it. However, the future goes to those who go boldly and courageously into an uncertain future, looking to weave the best of the past into the bright prospects of a different kind of future. The classroom of the future will hardly be a classroom at all. It will be a collection of activities that engage the learner from the inside out instead of from the outside in. Whatever emerges that aligns with the needs of a different kind of society and economy, it will not be just reforming and improving what already exists to make it more efficient, it will be a complete rethinking and redesign of what learning means and how learning occurs. This design will be based on transformational learning and Future Forward Colleges.

All colleges and institutions are fundamentally in the business of workforce development, whether the student is studying for a certificate in HVAC or a PhD in Astrophysics. At the same time, there will be a rebirth of a new concept for "liberal arts" as the skills of insight, intuition, innovation and imagination become key for a new type of entrepreneurial economy.

Educating a Future Forward Workforce

We are in the early stages of an economic shift so significant, based on networks and complex adaptive systems, that a new form of organization will evolve that will be neither capitalism nor socialism as we know it. It is with this emergence of a new type of economy in mind that the following framework is suggested to establish a 21st century workforce for the (emerging) Creative Molecular Economy. This new type of workforce will need the capacity to innovate, collaborate at a deeper level, and be capable of adapting to constant change in a fast-paced, increasingly complex society using communications technology and a new way of thinking. For any local workforce to prepare for an economy in constant change, we need a systemic approach. Individuals will become responsible for their own economic capacities and will need the following:

- An understanding of how the society is transforming and how this transformation will impact economic opportunities for themselves and their communities.
- Lifelong learning skills, as individuals learn how to spot emerging weak signals and develop the capacity as entrepreneurs to create new opportunities for income streams from different sources.
- Capability to be constantly innovative by developing the capacity to connect total disparate idea spaces into new products and services that adapt to changing conditions.
- Capability to use Internet access in multiple ways, to include uploading blueprints for new products that can be

custom manufactured at instant manufacturing sites and shipped within the week to individuals anywhere in the world.

- Well-developed imagination, intuition, and insight, so that individuals can be a part of a creative workforce able to adapt to constant change.
- Ability to connect with other people and organizations throughout the world to develop innovation networks around emerging ideas, issues, or opportunities.

Emerging across the country are bold and innovative methods of approaching higher education, known by various names, such as Transformational Learning and Future Forward College, which has been originated at Wake Tech Community College in North Carolina. These efforts don't nibble around the edges; they bite off the whole cookie. They are aimed at helping students learn differently, faster and with more relevance to the needs of a creative workforce.

How are these efforts different from long-standing methodologies? One good sign that transformational (disruptive) efforts are happening is that a new language has sprung up to explain its concepts. Do you remember before we used to "just Google it." New language springs up to explain transformational ideas and functions.

In this new transformational effort, there are several innovative concepts that are slowly making their way into the collective conscious of higher education educators. Below are short definitions of each concept.

- Trans-disciplinary learning: connecting disparate ideas as a result of identifying emerging weak signals and new trends. This type of learning will emphasize holistic thinking within a futures context.
- Complex Adaptive Systems: looking at nature to see how

natural things are organized and use those theories (such as chaos, complexity, and ecology) to create, organize and transform what we do today to insure that what is designed is aligned to be able to adapt to a different kind of society and economy that continues to emerge.

- Adaptive planning: An alternative to strategic planning, which is based on targeting specific outcomes that were defined before any planning processes were begun. This was appropriate when society changed slowly enough to deploy long-term plans based on a more efficient approach to existing ideas and methods. In a new world of exponential change, we need to plan for quick and responsive changes in real time as any situation changes and as new opportunities arise.

- Adaptive and traditional strategic planning can be layered together in a parallel or blended process that achieves explicit goals in the short run while insuring creative innovations in order to adapt to changing circumstances.

- And/both Parallel Processes: as we plan for transformation, we will not be able to throw the baby out with the bathwater. We need to be able to create new concepts and methods of transformational learning as the older, more traditional methods of learning lag into shorter and shorter life cycles. Each will be needed, in parallel, in this time of transition.

- Identify weak signals: we need to recognize emerging bits of new knowledge that are precursors to strong emerging trends. We must guide to the future and not teach to the past.

- Master Capacity Builders: this is the leadership ability to focus on building capacities for transformation and dealing with emerging issues not previously experienced. It complements traditional "project leadership" with a new leadership framework that is able to anticipate the future as opposed to looking to the past for solutions to more complex issues.

- Unlearning and Uplearning: learning to let go of old wisdoms that no longer apply, and to think and act at a higher level of complexity.
- Self-Directed Learning: we need to learn what we want, when we need it. Shift away from prescribed courses to learning experiences that are hyper-individualized.
- Interdependency: move from independence to interdependence as the norm. Teach students to understand how to look to the future for context as well as look for connections in emerging knowledge.

Key Elements of a Future Forward College

The following identify and define important ideas contained in the framework of a Future Forward College. When considered as a whole, a system of Transformational Learning is in the process of emerging.

We have grouped these innovations into three categories:

1 Evolving Teaching Methodology
2 Evolving Tools
3 Emerging processes, networks and mindsets

Evolving Teaching Methodology

Facilitating Hyper-Individualized Curricula

Learning what we want, when we want it – shifting away from a prescribed course agenda to one that is hyper-individualized, self-selected, and scheduled at times that sync well with the student will dramatically change levels of motivation and participation. Since each student comes with his/her own unique mixture of skills, desires, and preferences, the sooner a student can focus in on the

traits and talents they excel at, the quicker they will be able to find a meaningful direction for themselves.
Thomas Frey, DaVinci Institute, Louisville, CO

Learning Guide/Learning Engineer

As personalized learning becomes the norm over time, the role of a teacher will shift from providing content to new forms helping individuals identify what knowledge modules and other emerging skills will be important for the future ... whether it is preparing for new jobs, or learning how to be an effective citizen in a constantly changing world. "Schools" will be redefined and learning guides/engineers will collaborate with students in many non-traditional ways. One key role will be to become a "membrane penetrator" that links individuals and collaborating learning networks to the real world.

The membrane between the real world and all of its marvels, opportunities and problems, and our schools will become transparent.
Jon Madian, Building Our 21st Century Learning Community.

Value-Added or Connective Listening

This is an emerging capacity of a Master Capacity Builder, accelerated connector and learning engineer who understands the need to use existing and emerging knowledge as a way to form bridges of transformational thinking in students of all ages. A value-added listener looks to connect what is said to other information or knowledge in order to create an environment in which new ideas and innovations can emerge. The staple of a connective listener is to frame an effective question that can help a colleague, student or friend shift into a new paradigm by helping that person stop and go hmmm?

Cognitive Brain Research

In recent years, educators have explored links between

classroom teaching and emerging theories about how people learn. Exciting discoveries in neuroscience and continued developments in cognitive psychology have presented new ways of thinking about the brain – the human neurological structure and the attendant perceptions and emotions that contribute to learning. Explanations of how the brain works have used metaphors that vary from the computer (an information processor, creating, storing, and manipulating data) to a jungle (a somewhat chaotic, layered world of interwoven, interdependent neurological connections) (Southwest Educational Development Laboratory). Gerald Edelman, chairman of the Department of Neurobiology at Scripps Research Institute and 1972 recipient of the Nobel Prize for Physiology, offers a view of the brain that could influence the future of learning. Edelman's vision of the brain as a jungle in which systems interact continuously in a chaotic fashion suggests that learners would thrive in an environment that provides many sensory, cultural, and problem layers.

Targeted Learning

Targeting learning means you learn what you need to learn without wasting your time with what you may already know. Mentored Learning is an on-demand delivery model, you determine when you attend training and for how long. Each workstation contains two computer monitors. On one, you can access the course content: video, text and audio. On the other monitor, you have access to the production environment so you can practice your skills at any time during the course. This allows you to fast-forward through areas, or stop the content and practice a concept hands-on as many times as you need. This increases knowledge retention and the ability to apply your newly acquired knowledge on the job. Your learning path can then be customized to fill a specific skills gap. An individual is completely in charge of the pace of the course and the content covered so he/she can focus only on what they need to learn.

Modular Knowledge

The future of learning will not focus on extensive scope and sequence curricula. Instead it will be based on modules of emerging knowledge that can be connected to exiting knowledge modules. This approach will allow a constantly changing approach to 21st century core knowledge to be provided for any area of learning at the same time that a changing context within which that knowledge will be needed is seen as morphing. This approach will allow any student to work in collaboration with peers, mentors and learning guides anywhere in the world to create individualized curricula and new learning methodologies. Such an approach will give any student an understanding of the need to identify weak signals and emerging knowledge as the basis for constant individualized innovation.

History-Future Analogies

In a time of constant transformation, the knowledge and under-standing of context becomes critical. One of the great challenges when shifting thinking into new paradigms of the future is to help an individual come to his or her own conclusion that there is a need for change and to develop a capacity to transform him or herself. One of the ways in which this can be done is to utilize historical circumstances and stories to illustrate how our ancestors adapted to their own times of radical change, look for principles that are applicable to today, and utilize the connection of historical context and a futures context to help any individual learn why transformation is needed and how to adapt oneself, one's organization and one's community to an emerging future very different from the past.

Transformational Coach

There is no greater need in a Future Forward College or for the needs of community transformation than to have Master Capacity Builders who can provide the function and facilitation of a Transformational Coach. Important for developing capacities for transformation will be the capacity to help people see the need to shift their thinking into new paradigms, the capacity to design parallel processes to move transformation ahead in systemic ways, the capacity to ask appropriate questions, the capacity to connect disparate ideas, people, processes and projects, and the capacity to spot and utilize access points. All of these are key to the future vitality and dynamic sustainability of organizations and communities in a time of constant change. Without transformational coaches who are able to mentor others during times of challenge, no effective transformation will occur.

Access Points

A key skill for any learning guide, Transformational Leader, and Master Capacity Builder is to be able to identify an access point where a new idea, concept or method can be seeded in the thinking and activities of people, processes, organizations and communities. Whether it is a question someone asks, an existing need defined, or a concern expressed in confidence, multiple access points occur constantly and are key to transformational thinking and action.

Interdependency

Probably the most important ongoing historical transition is the shift from the core idea of independence to the idea of interdependence. In linear thinking, one looks for the best practice or one best idea. In non-linear, systemic thinking, there is a need to look to identify how multiple factors interconnect. Thus, it is important to understand the shift, in this time of immense change, from the core concept of independence to one of interdependence. One of the key impacts of this is to transform the education system to help students learn how to understand context and how to look for connections in knowledge and ideas that are emerging in order to be creative and innovative and not just efficient.

Uplearning

This is the capacity to think at a higher level of complexity, connect disparate ideas in real time and an ability to work with ecosystems. In the future an educated person will require all three capacities and a sense of how to seed new ways of thinking in oneself and others in order to help build an environment for continuous transformation.

Tools

Smart Mobile Devices

Smart mobility will change the way people interact. Increasingly, smart devices — portable tools that connect to the Internet — have become a part of our lives. In the last quarter of 2010, sales of smartphones outpaced those of PCs for the first time, according to data from IDC. In 2016, more smart devices will be used to access the Internet than traditional PCs. The move to an increasingly mobile world will create new players and new opportunities for a variety of industries. *"We expect that new emerging market companies will be significant competitors, growing rapidly in part because a lack of legacy systems will enable them to profit more quickly from any new technology as it becomes available. Emerging markets will create plenty of opportunities related to smart technology, and they will not be limited to for-profit enterprises."*
Ernst & Young

Gamification

Gamification is a process that engages people's instincts for learning and socialization, sometimes just for fun and at other times for rewards and points in competitive challenges. In learning focused gamification, tutorial and story based modules are created to resemble games. Sometimes people compete against their fellow students and other times one is competing with oneself.

Futures Generative Dialogue

Futures Generative Dialogue can be defined as the process of interaction, based on "connective listening," which helps to create new ideas, concepts and methods within a constantly changing context. It replaces the idea of debate, discussion and even traditional dialogue, and builds on new connections that can be developed when new trends, weak signals, and transformational ideas about the future are integrated into the dialogue. By definition, this type of dialogue opens up new thinking. Often, the most important outcomes of Futures Generative Dialogue are those things that could not have been anticipated when entering the dialogue.

Adaptive Planning

It doesn't just seem that the world is changing faster and that volatility is greater than it used to be. Both are measurably and demonstrably true, and both emerge from our increasingly connected economy. Our institutions, businesses included, have been built for stability, not for change. As connectivity proceeds, business leaders face an imperative to create organizations that can adapt continually and rapidly, to keep pace with shifts in their markets, technologies, and society itself.

It is the world of biology that holds the key to meeting that adaptive imperative. Adaptation, the process by which organisms respond to volatility in their environments, has been going on for the past four billion years. As businesses today are struggling with volatility, they can look to nature's example for lessons on adaptation.

Stan Davis and Christopher Myer, *It's Alive: The Coming Convergence of Information, Biology and Business.*

21st Century Technologies

The emphasis on STEAM knowledge (science, technology, engineering, arts and math) is just beginning. In the future, a more complex society will require citizens and a workforce who are more knowledgeable and capable of dealing with systems and integrated thinking than ever before. The following technologies will be at the center of any successful organization and community: advanced computerization and deep data; renewable energies to include solar and wind; composite materials; nanotechnology; biotechnology; artificial intelligence and cognitive brain and medical technologies.

Semantic Web 3.0

The Web is entering a new phase of evolution. There has been much debate recently about what to call this new phase. Some would prefer to not name it at all, while others suggest continuing to call it "Web 2.0". However, this new phase of evolution has quite a different focus from what Web 2.0 has come to mean. Web 3.0, a phrase coined by John Markoff of the *New York Times* in 2006, refers to a supposed third generation of Internet-based services that collectively comprise what might be called 'the intelligent Web" — such as those using semantic web, microformats, natural language search, data-mining, machine learning, recommendation agents, and artificial intelligence technologies — which emphasize machine-facilitated understanding of information in order to provide a more productive and intuitive user experience. There are actually several major technology trends that are about to reach a new level of maturity at the same time. The simultaneous maturity of these trends is mutually reinforcing, and collectively they will drive the third-generation Web. From this broader perspective,

Web 3.0 might be defined as a third-generation of the Web enabled by the convergence of several key emerging technology trends: Broadband adoption, Mobile Internet access, Mobile devices, Software-as-a-service business models, Web services interoperability, Distributed computing (P2P, grid computing, hosted "cloud computing" server farms such as Amazon S3), Semantic Web technologies (RDF, OWL, SWRL, SPARQL, Semantic application platforms, and statement-based datastores such as triplestores, tuplestores and associative databases), Distributed databases — or what is called "The World Wide Database" (wide-area distributed database interoperability enabled by Semantic Web technologies), Intelligent applications (natural language processing, machine learning, machine reasoning, autonomous agents). Web 3.0 will be more connected, open, and intelligent.

Futures Institute/Futures Station

Every community will need to have a central locale where futures thinking and transformational design is the focus for preparing for a different kind of economy and society. Included in a "futures institute" or "futures station" will be the need for cutting edge communications technology, areas for futures generative dialogue, areas for 21st century entrepreneurs to connect, and learning spaces to build capacities for transformation in the thinking, attitudes and behavior of as many citizens as possible.

Virtual Reality/Augmented Reality

Virtual Reality (VR) becomes a substantial and ubiquitous technology and subsequently penetrates applications for education, learning and training. In addition to multimedia, VR places the user in a three dimensional environment. The user feels in the middle of another environment. Most of the VR systems allow the user to travel and navigate. More promising for learning purposes is to let the user manipulate objects and experience the consequences. Augmented reality occurs when the user faces the real world, but on top of that the VR environment superimposes a computer-generated message in order to assist the user to perform the right operations. Educational VR systems seem to be a natural extension of computer-based simulations nowadays. The basic approach is to allow students to explore and discover the fundamental laws in a new environment and domain. "The ultimate dream is to merge the real world and the virtual world into a totally seamless experience," according to the PhotoSynth project. The next step (2016-2020) is going to be development of more open systems, where content can be moved across platforms and where separate worlds can be linked. For example, a room in a virtual building can be simulated on a private server using different simulation software.

Emerging Processes, Networks and Mindsets

Creating Interactive, Parallel Process, Ping-Pong Effects

When designing a system of parallel processes for systemic transformation, it is important to realize that key transformational elements, to include emerging new knowledge, will be determined by how many people and ideas outside an organization and community are connected into the thinking and action of local change efforts. External "Ping-Pong" effects are created that introduce local citizens to emerging weak signals and transformational thinking. This helps to evolve totally new ideas as a part of a national/international ecosystem of people and organizations.

Benchmarking Continuous Transformation

The concept of benchmarking continuous transformation is not focused on that which already exists but that which is emerging. Therefore, to benchmark that which only is beginning to appear needs an ability to re-conceptualize the idea of benchmarking.

Continuous Improvement takes an idea, concept, process or product and improves it, refines it or enhances what already exists. Therefore when benchmarking continuous improvement, one seeks to increase efficiency.

Continuous Innovation combines the ideas of efficiency and creativity. The ideas may have been around for a while, but the ways they are connected in an act of creativity is different. In this case, benchmarking balances the ability to spot what are best practices while adding a creative spark that introduces an innovation that could not have developed without a new way to combine existing ideas, methods or products. Wii is an example due to the connection of a digital gaming with the principle of an accelerator of a car.

Continuous Transformation focuses only on the act of constant creativity that introduces distinctly different elements that did not exist before. As a result, the concept of benchmarking continuous transformation is always looking at the horizon for newly emerging weak signals that previously have never existed. To benchmark the web in 1994 was to think about how such an idea could be used to change the undergirding principles of various aspects of society and the economy. Examples of such an approach would be the use of the Web to eliminate the middle man (disintermediation), to eliminate the physical retail function, or to transform the very nature of medicine.

Analogous Complexity

The purpose of analogy in science education is to effect conceptual change: specifically in terms of a new or altered understanding. Of course, not everything that is to be learned or understood as a result of the analogical process will always pre-exist in the learner's cognition. There will be occasions when new data needs to be processed for learning to occur.

Dr. Yvette Hancock & Dr. Andrys Onsman, Monash University.

This concept of analogous complexity will become a core way for learning guides to help students see systemic connections in multiple ideas, people and processes. For example, an understanding of the biomicracy of nature is central to understanding the methods of interdependency in a society, and leads to the skill of designing parallel processes and ecosystems.

Identifying Weak Signals

Weak Signals are precursors to full-blown trends at some later stage...
Elina Hiltunen (Finland).

Weak signals are emerging ideas, inventions, discoveries and innovations that are not yet trends, but have the potential to impact local areas within three to five years. Weak signals can inform any process through which learning is focused on adapting to a different future. How do you identify weak signals that lead to the next big thing?

There's no substitute for being in the habit of looking for ideas and working with them once they're found. Perhaps the mother of these habits is to simply be interested in the world around you—and attentive to its varied possibilities
Andy Boynton, Dean of the Boston College Carroll School of Management

Chaos, Complexity and Ecology

The study of how living and nonliving things organize themselves into patterns and interact as systems. Complexity is extremely multidisciplinary and involves scientists in a vast assortment of fields from Biology to Physics. It is also closely related to Fractal Geometry and Chaos Theory. Chaos is a scientific theory for dealing with systems that are complex, unpredictable, and/or have random events. In other words, most of the real world. Natural systems are so complicated that no matter how carefully we measure them, we can't know everything about them. Although measurements can be extremely accurate, they can't be accurate to infinity, and tiny differences/errors in the beginning can lead to gigantic ones later. This is known as the Butterfly Effect, because under the right circumstances, the effect of the fluttering of a butterfly's wings can make the difference between whether or not there will be a tornado.(So much for ever getting accurate weather predictions.) This shows how even the actions of the smallest creature (individual) can have a large effect on the whole. In ecological systems, everything is connected.

Wikipedia

Science of Networks

We are witnessing an increasing awareness that if we are to tackle complexity, the tools to do so are being born right now, in front of our eyes. The field that benefited most from this data windfall is often called network theory, and it is fundamentally reshaping our approach to complexity. Born at the twilight of the twentieth century, network theory aims to understand the origins and charac- teristics of networks that hold together the components in various complex systems. By simultaneously looking at the World Wide Web and genetic networks, Internet and social systems, it led to the discovery that despite the many differences in the nature of the nodes and the interactions between them, the networks behind most complex systems are governed by a series of fundamental laws that determine and limit their behavior.

Albert Laszlo-Barabosi, Notre Dame University, author of Linked.

Future Basics

When the term basics is utilized for education, the traditional tendency is to think of reading, writing, computer skills and traditional critical thinking. Although these skills will continue to be important to any individual, the future is changing so rapidly that the concept of what is basic is no longer taken for granted and fully understood. In a time of constant change and radical transformation of our society and economy, new ideas and skills will become basic to the context of any person involved in life-long learning. It is not just knowledge that exists that needs to be learned, but how emerging knowledge and new skills, never before needed, will become basic to our society. New sciences and technologies include biotechnology, nanotechnology and advanced computerization plus the capacity to rethink fundamental ideas about how learning occurs, how to connect totally disparate ideas, and focusing on developing the capacities for insight, intuition, imagination and constant innovation.

2020 Professions

In 2000, a number of futurists proposed that 40% of the professions and jobs that existed in 2020, would evolve from technologies that did not exist in 2000. Some of those suggested are social media manager, mobile application developer, composite materials specialist, personal robot repairman, accelerated network connector, home biotechnician, mobile collaborative governance coordinator, cloud cartel big data technologist, etc....
Hewlett Packard blog.

All students will need to develop the capacity to identify emerging weak signals and trends to determine how to develop new skills that will be in demand and learn how to monetize those skills effectively in ways that will create multiple income streams as a result of continuous innovation.

Social Networks

The future impact of social networking has just begun. Mark Suster, venture capitalist at GRP Partners predicted eight trends in December 2010:

- The social graph will become portable,
- We will form around true social networks: Quora, Hackernews, Namesake,
- Privacy issues will continue to cause problems,
- Social networking will become pervasive: Facebook Connects meets Pandora, NY Times,
- Third party tools will embed social features in websites,
- Social networking (like the Web) will split into layers such as SimpleGEO, PlaceIQ,
- Social chaos will create new business opportunities i.e., Klout, Sprout Social, CoTweet, awe.sm, (next gen) Buzzd, and
- Facebook will not be the only dominant player.

Emerging Connections and Disconnections

In an age of constant change and interlocking networks, the concept of emerging connections and disconnections of diverse ideas, processes, people, projects, etc., will be at the core of any local community's capacity to adapt to changing conditions. The following examples reflect this emerging trend in the realm of education: Blended learning in the liberal arts and blending on-line and classroom learning (Bryn Mawr). Also the Components of Connectivism: At its core, George Siemens' theory of connectivism is the combined effect of three different components: chaos theory, importance of networks, and the interplay of complexity and self-organization (University of Georgia School of Education).

Non-Linear Systems

We are moving from an age of linear, deterministic thinking to one of non-linear, self-organizing, emergent connections of people, ideas and processes. The capacity to identify, understand and work with non-linear systems will become key for communities interested in adapting to changing conditions as well as for a workforce able to innovate continuously. Non-linear systems and processes do not present the familiar bell-shaped distribution associated with linear systems, where change is gradual and orderly and where measurements crowd together near an average value. On the contrary, Mandelbrot, and Gleick amongst others, discovered that in non-linear systems change is more random and less predictable, and it involves discontinuities and Black Swan events. Examples of non-linear systems are: weather systems: ecology systems: global, financial systems; gardens; evolution of a more complex society.

Global Innovation Networks

A global knowledge economy is emerging in which the winners will be those who can successfully manage a global network of partners with access to technology, capabilities and local market understanding.
(Booz & Co).

In the emerging Creative Molecular Economy, global innovation networks will become more entrepreneurial as individuals, small groups and corporations will connect and disconnect in a dance of continuous innovation and transformation. "Corporations around the world are racing to develop breakthrough new products and gain a competitive advantage. They're looking for new technologies from the outside to speed the process," said Andy Zynga, CEO of NineSigma, the leading innovation partner to organizations worldwide. *"This drive to innovate is providing opportunities for entrepreneurs to be matched with organizations from other geographic regions or industries who have an immediate need for their solutions, and are willing to pay for them."* This matchmaking is at the heart of open innovation, which involves connecting organizations with the world to accelerate new solution development. Entrepreneurs are climbing onto the open innovation bandwagon to develop new business opportunities associated with this increasingly popular strategy.

Interlocking Community Networks

During the past thirty years the focus for community-based planning has been the concept of strategic planning that brings leaders of communities together to agree on a unified approach to preparing for the future, based on targeted outcomes and use of project teams to meet those outcomes with accountability schedules predetermined. The future of community planning will be very different due to the inability to predict the future and determine specific outcomes at some point in the future. As a result, adaptive planning will utilize the method of creating core groups of early adaptors around emerging transformational ideas and developing interlocking community networks. These networks will self-organize depending on the needs of any situation to include 21st century learning groups, futures projects and contests and community events.

Connective Thinking

A key to the future of 21st century learning is to help all students develop the capacity for connective thinking. Such a skill will insure that whatever a student learns, he or she is always looking to consider how a newly emerging idea can connect to something else to create an innovation of business, community transformation or individual service. The term "mashup" has evolved in the last decade to reflect this skill of connecting totally disparate ideas. Examples of connective thinking are Wii, Fluid Fabric

Systems, and Mobile Collaborative Governance.

Futures Appreciative Inquiry

The concept of Appreciative Inquiry (AI) has been utilized as a mechanism for positive change for many years. Only recently has the use of appropriate questions been considered as a way to help build capacities for transformation in people, organizations and communities. When considering a time in the future that has no template or model by which to go, statements of existing facts are not possible, questions become a key vehicle to help others think about ideas and concepts that are only beginning to be discernable and have possible patterns emerging. Examples of such questions are:

1) what if we...?
2) did you see the article...?
3) how might we connect...?

Any leader and facilitator of new ways of learning will need to become skilled at asking appropriate questions to help others come to see the need to shift thinking into new paradigms.

The Concept of Holism in education

The highest function of education is to bring about an integrated individual who is capable of dealing with life as a whole.
J. Krishnamurti

Unlearning

In a time of great change, what has been considered truth is no longer valid in many cases. The capacity to "unlearn" what has worked in the past, is one of the greatest needs of modern man and woman. It is important to realize that unlearning requires a quiet confidence, maturity and true humbleness to create an environment of "efficient unlearning."

Consider the following poem by an 11th century monk mentioned in Jack Uldrich's book, Unlearning 101.

When I was a young man, I wanted to change the world.

I found it was difficult to change the world, so I tried to change my nation.

When I found I couldn't change the nation, I began to focus on my town. I couldn't change the town and as an older man, I tried to change my family.

Now, as an old man, I realize the only thing I can change is myself, and suddenly I realize that if long ago I had changed myself, I could have made an impact on my family. My family and I could have made an impact on our town. Their impact could have changed the nation and I could indeed have changed the world.

Biomimicry

If chaos theory transformed our view of the universe, biomimicry is transforming our view of life on Earth. Biomimicry is innovation inspired by nature – taking advantage of evolution's 3.8 billion years of R&D since the first bacteria. Biomimics study nature's best ideas: photosynthesis, brain power, and shells – and adapt them for human use. They are revolutionizing how we invent, compute, heal ourselves, harness energy, repair the environment, and feed the world. Biomimicry has a great potential for helping students learn systemic, ecological thinking and how to adapt.

Continuous Innovation

The ability to create an environment that supports continuous innovation is a great challenge when the culture of local communities is still based on the ideas of standard answers, linear thinking and strategic planning. Only by developing the capacities in people, organizations and communities to search for new ideas and be open to change in general will we develop a truly adaptable workforce, economy and society able to be vital and successful in a time of radical transformation.

Biological Organization

During the Industrial Age, as we learned to analyze what existed, the principles of physics predominated. In the future, as the Ecological Civilization emerges, biological principles come to the forefront of importance because of the need to think systemically, understand how complexity evolves, and how to see connections among totally disparate ideas, processes, people and events. The idea of dynamic, interlocking networks and collaborating ecosystems will replace the structure of rigid hierarchies as the building blocks of our society and economy.

New 21st Century Literacy

Alvin Toffler, a famous futurist is quoted as saying, *"The illiterate of the 21st century will not be those who cannot read and write but those who cannot learn, unlearn and relearn."* The Center for Communities of the Future would add the concept of the need for "uplearning" to be literate in the 21st century. Bill Crossman in California believes that by the year 2040, computer artificial intelligence will interact with humans through voice synthesization, and thus reading as a skill will not be needed. In any event, what it means to be literate in the future will have elements of the past, but will require different skills that will allow individuals to be productive citizens in a more complex world and economy.

The ability to evaluate the outcomes of students who graduate from a Future Forward College will in itself need to transform from testing content to demonstrating impact on the community. The following page offers expected outcomes and strategies, and potential community impact as a result of designing a FFC 21st Century Transformational Learning Team.

21st Century Transformational Learning Teams will combine futures thinking with action to build capacities for transformation in local areas.

Transformational Learning

Strategy proposal worksheet

Seeding Community Transformation

Emerging Idea, Weak Signal, Discovery	Potential Impact
Education: Establish a Future Forward College Team	By developing the ability to build transformational skills and capacities in its students, community colleges will be able to help prepare students of all again to adapt to a constantly changing society and economy.

Strategy For Building Capacities:

1 Establish a core group of Deans and Division Heads to become Master Capacity Builders.
2 Create a Future Forward College Workbook to be used as a guide.
3 Establish a Center for Strategic Futures that can be utilized as a parallel platform to develop new projects for a FFC.
4 Have modular certification established for core skills and capacities for Future Basics.
5 Develop interlocking networks of students interested in helping to position the FFC at the forefront of learning for community colleges.

Expected Outcomes:

1 Students will be able to understand the ongoing transformation in society.

2 A culture of "futures thinking" will be developed in the college through the development of a new concept of learning guide.

3 Students will be able to identify emerging professions and prepare for them.

4 Virtual learning will become the norm.

5 Students will be able to engage in transformational thinking and action by asking appropriate questions and connecting disparate ideas.

Chapter 4

Building a Creative Molecular Economy

(Transforming Economic Development)

In a simple linear system, say one bank and one farm, you can map out the effects of a crisis as if you were plotting the route of falling dominoes. But in a networked society, lit up by revolutionary change, such easy prediction is a fantasy.

Resilience allows us, even in the most extreme moments, to keep learning, to change. It is a kind of battlefield courage, the ability to innovate under fire because we've prepared in the right way and because we've developed the strength to keep moving even when we're slapped by the unexpected. But resilience has to be built into our system in advance, like a strong immune response before flu season. In practice this means widening how we interact with the world – the better to learn new skills and make new connections – instead of narrowing to the fewest possible essential threats or plans or policies.

The Age of the Unthinkable, Joshua Cooper Ramo

In his book, *The Age of the Unthinkable,* Joshua Cooper Ramos identifies five ideas that will be necessary for any society dealing with constant change to prepare for a different kind of future. One of them is resilience, the ability to learn how to adapt systemically to constant shocks and constant change. He also talks about seeing things differently and holistically, not focused on one idea or one best practice. His concept of "indirectness," is important as is thinking differently and radically. Finally, creating distributive intelligence in the community.

We live in an age of such significant change that the very worldview we have used for two hundred years is in the process of transforming. Additionally, we believe that this transformation is structurally changing our economy and society and has profound implications for the practice of economic development.

Adding to the complexity over the next twenty years is the fact that there are three different types of economies that are in churn and mixed together for the first time in the history of the world.

The first is the very last stages of the old Industrial Age Economy based on hierarchies, economies of scale, mechanization, and predictability. The second is a transitional economic phase called the Knowledge Economy that was recognized a decade or so ago, and is based on knowledge creation and diffusion.

This transition phase is reaching its maturity and will quickly shift within the next ten-to-fifteen years to an emerging Creative Molecular Economy (CME) in which biological principles will form the framework for how the CME will be organized and operate.

What we mean by biological principles is human engineered systems that are dynamic, evolve, strive for equilibrium and have rhythms that are expected to grow, mature and change. This is in stark contrast to command and control systems based on authority, a one way to do things mentality and usually a highly regimented bureaucracy.

This newly emerging economy will flow with the speed and strength of a surging river, constantly overflowing the banks of traditional economic principles and thinking. In preparing for success in this new economy, we will need to have leaders in communities who are open to new ideas and begin to understand the challenges they face in transforming their approach to the future systemically – how they connect ideas, people, processes and methods; how they develop a culture in support of continuous innovation; how they build new capacities for a new type of economic development involving as many citizens as possible with distributive intelligence; how they create an environment for individualized, autonomous education/ learning; how they shift paradigms of governance using mobile technologies – and the list goes on and on.

What has become obvious is that we are in a time of comprehensive societal and economic transformation – and only by systemic approaches will we be able to adapt to an increasingly fast-paced, interconnected and complex society and economy. Minor reform of current systems and thinking will not get the job done. With only a true transformation to an economic system that is based on creativity, resiliency and interlocking entrepreneurs, will local areas be able to develop a vibrant and sustainable economy that will be able to adapt to constantly changing conditions that will be moving at exponential speed, thus a Creative Molecular Economy.

As a result of the rise of exponential change during this time of social and economic transition, the concept of economic development for local communities is in a period of transformation that is poorly understood by even the best of economic developers. Trained to think in linear terms and looking for best practices within the framework of industrial recruitment, economic developers are given the job of focusing all economic development through their authority, providing annual reports at the end of the year to those agencies responsible for funding local economic development.

Not only is this traditional approach increasingly obsolete, as many more jobs are created by individual entrepreneurs sharing knowledge and ideas over the Internet, the very concept of what economic development means in an increasingly fast-paced, interconnected and complex society and economy is transforming.

In an Industrial Economy, access to capital and location were key. In a Knowledge Economy, the ability to recruit creative people was central. In a Creative Molecular Economy, building organic economic resilience (developing distributed intelligence about the future economy throughout a local area as well as developing the skills for individuals and small groups to create their own 21st century entrepreneurial networks and innovation projects) in local communities will become the emerging focus for economic development. To do this, local leaders will need to become familiar with the concepts and methods of developing comprehensive community transformation.

Local leaders will be required to understand the core needs of each type of economy and be able to establish flexible methods and techniques to help local communities transform their thinking and actions as three parallel approaches (continue to recruit businesses from other areas of the U.S. and world, create an environment and culture to attract creative individuals, and seed new life science and networking capacities to begin to build a Creative Molecular Economy based on comprehensive community transformation) to economic development begin to complement each other. Individuals and organizations involved with economic development will need to understand how to create economic resilience in multiple ways, with organizations and individuals, creating a culture and environment that supports continuous innovation and transformation.

It is during this time of transition that professional economic developers will be caught in a Catch-22 situation. Their funding is provided by agencies whose decision makers see economic development as industrial recruitment only, and expect to hold those who receive money for economic development accountable based on predetermined outcomes. The concept of economic development is in the process of transforming from capital focused to creativity focused, from recruitment of industries to developing a culture of innovation, and from hierarchies, rules and best practices to connections, networks, and industries and jobs based on biological principles and methods. As a result, local economic developers and community leaders will be challenged to learn new theories and practices not a part of their traditional knowledge and experience in order to help seed capacities for community transformation that will support a new type of economy that is in the early stages of emerging.

We are currently in a "weak signal" stage of the next iteration of an economic system. This system demands local leaders who are able to shift their thinking and action back and forth among the current and rapidly changing future needs of business attraction and expansion (declining in importance over time); the development of a workforce capable of moving beyond continuous improvement to continuous innovation; the formation of individual collaborative connections and disconnections that form "innovation ecosystems" and many other interrelated challenges and opportunities to help new knowledge emerge. It will be the connection of new knowledge to new resources in the creation of transformational projects that will seed what we call a "Creative Molecular Economy,"* a term that is further explored and defined below:

Why Molecular? We use the term Creative Molecular Economy as a descriptive phrase to differentiate the emerging economy from the existing Industrial Economy and Knowledge Economy. Creative, in that new knowledge will always be disrupting the economy continuously. Molecular, in that individual entrepreneurs will collaborate in and through interlocking networks, co-creating products, service and ideas.

The Framework of a Creative Molecular Economy

Over the past thirty years the Creative Molecular Economy has been evolving as a result of the congruence of new technologies and the need to adapt quickly to market opportunities brought about by the transformation of the society. The characteristics and structure of a Creative Molecular Economy are very different from the previous Industrial Economy.

Below are defining ideas of a Creative Molecular Economy to include examples of where various elements are being developed. It will take twenty years for the Creative Molecular Economy to emerge fully, yet communities that do not realize the need to begin building capacities for a Creative Molecular Economy will find themselves so far behind they may never catch up.

- A broad-band infrastructure capable of uploading and downloading massive amounts of data and video-streaming.

Example: Only in Chattanooga, TN is 1 Gigabit-per-second internet speed available to every home and business – over 150,000 of them – throughout the entire community. Urban or rural, business or residence, internet speeds that are surpassed in the western hemisphere – from 50 megabits-per-second all the way up to 1 Gigabit-per-second are accessible here.

We have built an expansive, powerful, 100% fiber network. But the power isn't in the platform. The real power is in how we use it.

Our infrastructure spurs research and development of new technologies right here in the United States, and preserves American jobs.This is the ultimate tool for entrepreneurs. For established companies looking to become game-changers. For anyone needing a system that can help test and prove ideas.

Chattanooga Gig

- Electronic Entrepreneurism

Electronic Entrepreneurs have been a part of the Industrial Economy for over 100 years, beginning with Thomas Edison and the electric light bulb, to Thomas Watson and IBM's entrepreneurial development of computers to Steven Jobs, "the Father of the Digital World" who created the personal computer revolution. With the advent of the Web in the early 1990s, individuals for the first time could communicate with each other anywhere in the world. As a result, a myriad of connections of people, ideas and processes began to explode and the following key parts of a Creative Molecular Economy emerged.

- Building effective websites

Tim Berner-Law, an Englishman working at CERN in Switzerland, conceived the idea for HTML in 1989, thus providing the first software platform for computers to be able to add visual images to text. Over the twenty-six years, there has been an explosion of new types of software and hardware that now offer anyone the opportunity to build their own websites. Today there are hundreds of web development sites which offer any individual the opportunity to create a web presence for small fees or even for free ... such as Site Builder, Website Builder.com, & Sitey.

- Connecting Disruptive Technologies for Innovation

The Web allows individuals entrepreneurs to connect with other entrepreneurs to connect knowledge and expertise in the creation of new products and services. Often known as "disruptive" technologies, the emergence of "innovation ecosystems" are at the forefront of electronic entrepreneurism. Examples of newly emerging technologies important to electronic entrepreneurs are the Mobile Internet, Automation of Knowledge Work, the Cloud, the Internet of Things and 3-D printing.

Nanocorps and netpreneurs (Small ventures by entrepreneurs that rely on emerging technologies for an early market advantage).

An example of a new organizational concept aligned with the Creative Molecular Economy connects netpreneurs into a "collaborative Innovation ecosystem". Communities of the Future has created an initial prototype by designing three cells with three nodes in each cell. The original ecosystem included an economic development cell (Camoin Associates in Saratoga Springs, NY, Rose and Associates in North Carolina and the Center for Creative Living in Cedar Falls, IA), an educational cell (Wake Tech Community College in Raleigh, NC, Tarrant County College in Ft. Worth, TX, and University of the District of Columbia Community College in Washington, DC). COTF is the facilitator of this new Creative Innovation Ecosystem. Each organization plays a role in various aspects of the ecosystem.

• Continuous Transformation

One of the keys to the evolution of a vibrant and sustainable Creative Molecular Economy is to create an environment in which new ideas and creative processes are always at work. All Creative Innovation Ecosystems will be based on identifying emerging weak signals and designing futures generative dialogue processes that bring together "netpreneurs" from different fields of interest in order to insure innovative ideas evolve.

Continuous transformation is different from continuous improvement and continuous innovation in that it is focused only on newly emerging knowledge, ideas and methods that have not previously existed. In an age of constant change, the life cycles of ideas and products will be shorter and shorter, requiring networks of entrepreneurs to combine their knowledge, collaboration and research capability to develop new income opportunities.

- Connective, interdependent thinking

The concept of connecting thinking will become increasingly important as the society becomes more complex and innovation requires the connection of different ideas spaces. The book about Boulder, CO, Smart Communities, introduces the principle that emerged over twenty years that six Entrepreneurs from different fields is the optimum number to bring together for futures generative dialogue that results in new transformational products and services.

- Developing a futures context

We live in an age in which the emerging context of a Creative Molecular Economy is based on interlocking networks of creative people and organizations who learn to collaborate in the creative process. As the culture becomes more open and futures focused, there are more connections of ideas, people and processes that lead to research and development. From this search for new ways of thinking, and the connection of innovative and disruptive ideas, the content of products, ideas and methods are transformed. The advent of the Web in the early 1990s transformed all aspects of the economy and society within a decade.

- Recognizing new opportunities and creating ecosystems

The concept of "creative innovation ecosystems" is an emerging model aligned with the need to connect people, ideas and resources, not only to create innovations, but to also be able to adapt more quickly and spread new capacities faster. The use of the emerging Mobile Internet will give collaborative, creative individuals and groups a platform for quick innovation and funding to undergird start-up companies.

- Building Income Webs

In the past, individual entrepreneurs developed ideas and found partners to fund the innovation and build a company. In the future, networks of collaborators will develop new ideas and learn to design "income webs" that will work like DNA in a genetic sequence. Individuals will build deep knowledge in a particular area of the society and economy, and then work with other people in different parts of the world to seed the idea, method or technique at a cost much lower than in a traditional "job." By adding one's knowledge to multiple networks in different parts of the world, the revenue streams will insure that this type of 21st century entrepreneur (a netpreneur) will be able to have flexible time as well as income streams from involvement of different networks.

- The concept of building interlocking webs and networks

One of the ongoing transformations of the times is the use of Interlocking webs and networks to create research and development projects, access greater funding opportunities through crowdfunding, and building capacities for transformation among diverse people, organizations and communities. The ability to facilitate interlocking networks requires a new type of leader called a "master capacity builder" who understands how to identify emerging weak signals, how to spot access points to seed new ideas and processes, as well as learning how to create transformational ideas around which collaborating entrepreneurs can be drawn.

- Networking multiple nodes

Any "Creative Innovation Ecosystem" is designed around the principles used by nature. Any cell in nature is made up of three parts, the nucleus, the membrane and mitochondria. The use of biomimicry and biological principles is a key part of developing an effective and sustainable Creative Molecular Economy. The new Virtual Center for Economic Transformation is emerging as a collaboration among three nodes, diverse organizations in Iowa, New York and North Carolina. Each of these nodes has expertise in different areas Important to economic development. By connecting these nodes in collaboration, a new model for developing capacities for a Creative Molecular Economy is emerging.

- Core Futures Knowledge Blocks

One of the most important aspects of a Creative Molecular Economy is to insure that as many people and organizations as possible begin to realize that they need to develop futures thinking and futures action.

Emerging new knowledge is a key to innovation and transformation.

Any Creative Innovation Ecosystem needs to insure that different individuals become students of different areas of emerging technologies, design of ecosystems, and new human skills of leadership and learning.

- Transformational Leadership

There are two kinds of leadership, both of which will be needed in a time of constant change for different reasons. Project, or traditional leadership, focuses on the short-term and on strategic planning when resources and plans are already defined. The focus is on tangible outcomes that can be identified before any process is begun. Transformational Leadership is focused on the longer-term and emphasizes the ability to develop capacities for transformation to be able to adapt to changing situations.

- Identifying weak signals

Weak Signals is a term coined in the 1990s to designate an emerging technology, body of knowledge or skills that had not previous existed. Today, "creative innovation ecosystems" is a weak signal for leaders of organizational design who are stuck in the ideas and structure of an Industrial Society that emphasizes methods of strategic planning and a singular focus on outcomes. Too often, leaders try to take old ideas and make them more efficient, or take new ideas and force them into old processes of change based on strategic planning and not adaptive planning.

- Future trends and their impact

One of the most important parts of developing a core base of futures knowledge is to search for disruptive technologies and consider possible implications for one's organization and community.

The following identify ongoing trends in three key areas of society.

Health

The healthcare industry has a number of trends that will impact it over the next twenty years. One of the most important trends is the consolidation of small medical practices into larger conglomerates. The explosion of new technologies is quickly reconceptualizing the structure and practice of healthcare. In the future, paramedics and nurse practitioners will carry diagnostic technologies that can be used at bedside in homes. The emphasis is shifting from medicine by intervention to preventive medicine.

Business and Industry

There are many significant trends in business and industry. One of the most important is the use of artificial intelligence software to take the place of people in semi-creative jobs. When added to the increasing use of robots to replace humans in various fields to include manufacturing and medicine, the numbers of jobs will be reduced. In the past, new disruptive technologies created more jobs for humans than were lost, just at a higher level of skill. Thomas Frey, a well-known futurist and Director of the Davinci Institute in Colorado, predicts that by the year 2030, disruptive technologies will replace two billion jobs worldwide. A key challenge of the Creative Molecular Economy is to reconceptualize how the economy works in order to reconstitute the middle class.

Educational/Learning

Traditional education has focused on the content of knowledge. Broad and deep knowledge will be utilized to ask appropriate questions in order to create transformational ideas and methods. The future of learning with be based on identifying weak signals and connecting disparate ideas in a dance of constant creativity.

The present system of education at all levels was created to support an Industrial Age society and economy. In the future, a new learning framework and structure will emerge that will doom the end of the classroom, as individuals will inhabit the mobile web and learn from any place at any time.

- Disruptive Technologies

The following disruptive technologies will cause the reconceptualization of all society. One of the most important trends is the interconnectivity of different types of disruptive technologies to transform all aspects of humanity and society.

Communications/Computing

Cloud computing will be a catalyst to entrepreneurship — lowering both cost and logistical barriers to entry, as well as ushering in a new era of scalable businesses ranging from financial services to healthcare.

Biotechnology

The area of biotechnology is exploding with discoveries to include Materials Advances for Next-Generation Ingestible Electronic Medical Devices and non-GMO genetically edited crop plants.

Nanotechnology

Conceivably the most important disruptive technology that will impact all areas of life to include higher strength composite materials, improve nanoproduction to reduce costs, and nanomedicine.

- Adaptive Planning

Adaptive planning is a new approach for preparing for a

different kind of future in order to build capacities for transformation that enable people, organizations and communities to be able to adapt to changing conditions and situations.

Compared to Strategic Planning

Most older leaders have been trained in strategic planning. This method of preparing for the future assumes that one has the ability to identify specific outcomes before the process is begun, and control from the start to the finish in order to hold people accountable.

The SWOT (strengths, weaknesses, opportunities and threats) will still be utilized when resources are known, timeframes are defined and benchmarks are available. However, in a time of constant change, when one cannot predict any specific aspect of the future, the method of adaptive planning called DICE (design, identify, connect and emerge) is an effective way of using biological principles in the way that nature organizes evolution to be prepared for whatever emerges.

- Parallel Processes

In an emerging age of interdependent people, factors and ideas, the use of dynamic and transforming systems will be important. Since different parts of any non-static system evolves at different rates in different ways, the use of parallel processes becomes important. Any Creative Molecular Economy involving netpreneurs and innovation ecosystems will require designers and facilitators of parallel processes.

- Laying Seeds of Transformation

One of the most interesting and important aspects of building capacities for transformation is the ability to understand how to identify "access points" and how to seed new ways of transformational thinking and action. The concept of indirectness is a powerful method to create an environment in which others can come to the conclusion that they need to change. Seeds can be simple questions, a connection to a colleague in another part of the world, providing a link to a transformational website or developing a design team to rethink the role of a chamber executive.

- Concepts of Complex Adaptive Systems

Setting Initial Conditions

The design phase of transformational processes occurs when people are brought together for initial futures generative dialogue, or a network of organizations agree to become part of a new "creative innovation ecosystem."

Self-organization

Once a process is initiated, those involved are given the flexibility to build on the initial dialogue in any way that makes sense, whether inviting other people to participate, creating futures projects, etc.

Emergence

Instead of determining benchmarks and accountability schedules, a complex adaptive system is framed to allow new ideas, actions and outcomes to emerge from the interaction of those involved.

Feedback

One of the key aspects of a complex adaptive system is to insure feedback from both those involved in the process directly, as well as those external to the process that will be impacted by any decision that is made. If there is positive feedback, the process will gain momentum and scale. If there is enough negative feedback, the process will need to be adapted as a part of the concept of adaptive planning.

- Creativity Incubator

One of the most important factors when creating a culture of innovation in any community is to have a facility that allows people to have a safe space to dream and create together. Whether it is an innovation incubator or a futures station, the opportunity for thinking about the future without someone always saying why a new idea won't work will be a key to the success of any system for community transformation. Asheville, NC has created a "Collider" so that new ideas can bounce against each other in the spirit of a supercollider in physics.

Identifying emerging weak signal and trends

The ability to identify weak signals and emerging trends is one of the key factors in creating an environment for transformational thinking and action. This can be done through dialogue among peers and colleagues with great knowledge in different fields. It can also occur by having different people suggest websites that contain disruptive technologies and other emerging ideas important to the evolution of a Creative Molecular Economy.

Utilizing "futures generative dialogue"

The concept of futures generative dialogue is based on the idea that until ideas are considered within a futures context and a call to action occurs that leads to new capacities, there can be no transformation. Debate causes conflict and the lack of connections of people, ideas and processes so important to community transformation. Two people can discuss an issue, and never listen to each other. Dialogue provides an environment for people to interact, listen and ask questions, but can lead to obsolete conclusions if not set within a futures context.

Identifying income opportunities within a futures context

The creation of "apps" for mobile phones has become a huge industry. When augmented reality emerged a decade ago, real estate brokers enhanced their income opportunities by having any information or knowledge about the property accessible instantaneously.

Using a "concept paper" to frame a new idea

The Center for Communities of the Future uses the idea of bringing diverse colleagues together to collaborate to develop a concept paper. Most recently, a design team of chamber presidents from communities in different states came together in NC to develop a concept for rethinking the role of chambers as facilitators of "comprehensive community transformation."

- New ways to access capital for start-ups

The concept of crowdfunding will increase in importance for any individual, group or organization interested in developing a start-up business based on a new, innovative idea. Over the last decade hundreds of crowdfunding sites have been established to include Kiva, GoFundMe, Kickstarter, and Indiegogo. Any person, group or community that has a good idea can access capital from throughout the world using one or more of the crowdfunding sites.

The "great recession" of 2007-2009 has raised questions about the potential for increased economic volatility in the future. For economic developers and local leaders, however, there is a more fundamental question: "are we in the process of shifting from an Industrial Economy to a Creative Molecular Economy?" And, if so, how do we develop a new type of economic resiliency in our communities and society capable of adapting to constantly changing conditions. This resiliency cannot be achieved by just reforming the current practices of economic development. In other words, we can't just tinker at the margins. Economic development for a Creative Molecular Economy will need to be completely rethought.

Considering Economic Resilience in an Organic Age

So what in the world does it mean to talk about "economic resilience" in an Organic Age as a part of a Creative Molecular Economy (CME)? Let's start with a simple definition of a Creative Molecular Economy: "it is an economy based on the integration of emerging radical technologies, with creative individuals, small groups and companies organized in interlocking networks, connecting and disconnecting constantly in processes of continuous innovation."

Economic Resiliency in this type of economy is defined as: "motivating citizens to build capacities for transformation in a self-organizing way that connects individual creativity, global innovation networks, biological principles and adaptive planning in order to adapt to emerging opportunities and constant change."

Economic resiliency will take time to emerge as an idea that is understood by local leaders. The skills and methods necessary to support the creation of economic resiliency need to be seeded and evolved in the thinking and actions of leaders and citizens. The knowledge, persistence, patience and caring required of transformational leaders is important, especially in the initial stages of any community-based approach to transforming culture, a key aspect to any framework of economic resilience.

Throughout this book we have noted that different skills are necessary if we are to thrive fully in the 21st Century. To thrive, leaders must be nimble and open-minded thinkers who are comfortable working around the edges of tough issues. In addition, leaders must hold enough self-trust to allow their instincts to move into completely untried areas if a new pattern begins to emerge. And, it is critical that leaders empower people in the community/organization to engage on emerging problems to both tap into added brainpower and demonstrate transparency and trust.

These are very different values from the traditional leader and economic developer. As a result two things must happen for economic resiliency to emerge in any community. Any leader will need to learn how to shift back and forth between traditional methods and transformational approaches, depending on what is required for success, whatever success means as society and economies transform. Secondly, core groups and networks of leaders will need to form, interconnect and work in deeper collaboration.

What was once not understood, thought impossible, or ridiculed as ridiculous will morph to the acceptable norm as communities become adept at adaptive planning. A key initial step in the difficult journey will be to learn how to create resilience for a Creative Molecular Economy. Welcome to the paradox of The Age of the Unthinkable.

Seeding Economic Resiliency

Resilience is the capacity to absorb shocks to any system (in this case a community's economy) and constantly adapt to structures and processes that will evolve the economy and social structures in vital and sustainable ways. For this to occur, there are twelve concepts that need to be integrated into the thinking and actions of local communities:

- Shift the impetus for economic development from the

narrow concept of an economic developer to the entire community. Maintain the economic developer position to focus on industrial recruitment that is the strength of most economic developers.

- Establish a Futures Economy Council in the chamber of commerce to bring together a network of individuals interested in developing knowledge about a Creative Molecular Economy and seeding capacities in support of continuous innovation.

- Develop a website to focus and help build capacities for a CME to include a set of web-based resources.

- Create "interlocking networks" of citizens within the local area as well as with colleagues throughout the world to identify emerging ideas and new economic opportunities.

- Establish futures learning groups in collaboration with local libraries to seed new ways of thinking in the culture.

- Develop a community culture over a decade that is open to new ideas of any kind.

- Build core groups of transformational master capacity builders to help develop and network capacities for transformation.

- Provide a community-based approach to give incentives for all citizens who utilize the Internet to find new ideas and economic opportunities.
- Establish a Futures Institute at the local community college.

- Create a "Futures Communiversity" videoconference series for all interested citizens to have nationally known futurists and experts introduce transformational ideas and methods.

- Have citizens build relationships with startups, entrepreneurs and emerging notables to position local communities at the forefront of thinking for a Creative Molecular Economy.

- Develop local pilot programs, projects and events that illustrate some new Creative Molecular Economy idea or process.

- Develop a Future Forward Workforce initiative and become a part of a network of communities in the U.S. who are experimenting with the creation of a workforce that is aligned with the emerging Creative Molecular Economy.

A Future Forward Workforce

We are in the early stages of an economic shift so significant based on interlocking networks and complex adaptive systems, that a new form of organization will evolve that will be neither capitalism or socialism as we know it.

I see the emergence of social production and peer production as an alternative to both state-based and market-based closed, proprietary systems ... these activities can enhance creativity, production and freedom.
Yochai Benkler

The Wealth of Networks

The goal of communitarian technology (e.g Web 3.0) is this: to maximize both individual autonomy and the power of the people working together.
Kevin Kelly, *Wired Magazine*

By the year 2040, it is expected that 40-50 % of people will work from their homes (The Futurist Magazine). Within the next ten years, the traditional hierarchies of an Industrial Economy will continue to flatten and networks of people will continuously connect and disconnect, adapting to new economic opportunities. It is expected that the emerging Creative Molecular Economy will be undergirded by the principles of life science as what is made and how it is made is impacted by biological principles. Economic activity will reflect a mixture of large international firms organized in interlocking networks and complex adaptive systems, and individual 21st century entrepreneurs and small businesses, working in deeper collaboration with each other and with international organizations to create new products, services and experiences aligned with a different type of society and economy that is in the early stages of emerging.

In 1999, an eminent futurist, Marv Cetron, forecast that "within the next twenty years, the largest corporation in the world will have a staff no larger than 1500 people, whose roles it will be to design and facilitate networks and webs of core capabilities, free agents and start up companies."

Each local community will need to broaden and deepen the capacity of citizens to understand the emerging economic times that will be so different from the past, and prepare the thinking and action of an economic workforce in totally different ways. This will shift the emphasis of an economic developer in communities from recruiting industrial factories and businesses from other areas of the country and world, to building capacities for transformational thinking and action in order to create a culture of resiliency. A key factor in this will be creating a workforce able to adapt to a constantly changing economy that will be based on creativity, deeper collaboration and connectivity using human and computer skills.

Rethinking Criteria for a 21st Century Workforce

It is with this emergence of a new type of economy in mind that the following framework is suggested to establish a 21st century workforce for a Creative Molecular Economy, one that has the capacity to innovate, collaborate at a deeper level, and be able to adapt to constant change in a fast-paced society that is increasingly complex using communications technology and a new way of thinking:

Building Individual Capacities

For any local workforce to prepare for an economy in constant change, where competition will emerge from anywhere in the world, and when artificial intelligence will develop the capacity to do more than the most menial of tasks, a systemic approach must be taken. Individuals will become responsible for their own economic capacities and need to develop the following as previously mentioned.

1   An understanding of how the society is transforming and how this transformation will impact economic opportunities.

2   Lifelong learning will become more than a phrase as individuals learn how to spot emerging weak signals and their impact.

3   Individuals will learn how to be constantly innovative by connecting total disparate idea spaces.

4   Individuals will utilize access to the Internet in multiple

ways to include uploading blueprints for 3-D printing.

5   Individuals will need to learn how to develop their imagination, intuition and insight in order to develop continuous transformation.

6   Individuals will need to learn how to connect with other people and organizations to develop innovation networks.

7   Capital will be accessed from different sources worldwide through Crowdfunding.

- Building Community Capacities in Support of a Creative Molecular Economy Workforce

As the world economy becomes more interconnected, the traditional distinction between the needs of the individual and the needs of the community becomes a false dichotomy. For the first time in history self-interest and community interest are one because self-adaptive systems need to have individuals working in collaboration to create a culture that supports continuous innovation. The following are ways in which a community can create a culture of innovation:

1   Insure that there is universal access to dependable wireless or broadband infrastructure at a minimum of 10 Gb.

2   Have economic organizations such as the chamber of commerce, workforce initiatives and economic developers educate the community as to why it is important for a workforce to learn how to be involved in constant innovation and transformation using the skills of imagination, intuition and insight.

3   Build interlocking networks of all types for economic

resiliency to include connecting those under thirty who know how to utilize technology with those older who can share experiences to help the youth understand the context of how we arrived at this juncture in economic history.

4   Give incentives and awards for the most creative ideas and for those who understand how to build capacities for transformation in their communities as well as how to form innovation networks within and without the local region.

5   Establish a Future Economy Council in the community.

6   Develop a new type of leadership development whose graduates understand the theory and application of networks, who can identify trends and weak signals, and who can design parallel processes to help establish a culture in support of continuous innovation.

7   Establish a "21st century neighborhood academy network" in the community to seed Transformational Learning abilities in order for citizens to see patterns in an emergent situation and learn how to imagine totally new ideas.

Initial Conditions, Weak Signals and Trends

In the application and practice of chaos/complexity/ecology theory to emerging situations in early stages of development, there is a concept called "framing initial conditions." This early stage of a weak signal (such as the emergence of a Creatived Molecular Economy whose patterns are not fully recognized) reflects an ability to imagine possibilities without the need to target specific outcomes that cannot be assured as any new system evolves. One of the most important ideas for any 21st century practitioner of economic development is to understand that traditional practices of strategic planning limit one's ability to adapt to changing conditions. There are two assumptions of strategic planning. First, that one can predict the specific outcomes that need to be achieved. Second that one can control the processes to get from where one is to where one wants to be. Neither of these assumptions are valid in a time of constant change where ambiguity and uncertainty are the core attributes of any emerging system.

At the initial stages of a dialogue about the emergence of a Creative Molecular Economy, all participants look to identify ideas, methods and techniques that they think may be important to seed and evolve this new type of economy. In the early stages of any process of dialogue about a weak signal, it is as if thinkers were trying to connect fireflies darting about.

With this in mind, the following are miscellaneous and diverse ideas, discoveries and efforts that seem to have relevance to the evolution of a Creative Molecular Economy. These will be considered to be weak signals and trends that set initial condition for what we call "futures generative dialogue" when considering the emergence of a Creative Molecular Economy framework:

- As the costs of change become the regular costs of doing business, people's roles in organizations are shifting from doing work to managing the evolution of human and organizational capacities, whether by creating new software, new relationships or new ideas.

- The basic characteristics of weak signals are: 1) unique and not repeating, 2) without a history and time sequences, the evolution of weak signals is difficult to understand, 3) weak signals look ridiculous when they first appear, and

4) weak signals are often invisible to the experts.

• Across industries and regions, firms are abandoning vertically integrated innovation approaches in favor of Innovation Networks and Innovation Ecosystems, global partner ecosystems that co-develop and co-market new products, services, and business models.

• The molecular corporation is one that has a core coordinating function, yet incorporates free agents and small groups globally as a part of interlocking networks that are constantly being added and changed to provide research and development, production and marketing abilities.

An Act of Rethinking

The Creative Molecular Economy will evolve within a context of megatrends that will both impact and be impacted by ideas and factors that are just beginning to emerge. Whether facing the challenge of global warming, cultures in conflict, society reorganized utilizing innovation ecosystems or an increase in pace and complexity, those involved with economic development will need to rethink how to prepare local communities for a society in constant change where old models are outdated and weak signals are often met with ridicule and the cry for show me something practical.

For those interested in helping to identify emerging patterns associated with a Creative Molecular Economy, it is only necessary to think about the early '90s and remember how so many people paid no attention to the evolution of the Web. Within ten years, any organization or community that did not build electronic infrastructure capacity, realized that they were not economically competitive. Those who did not ridicule this weak signal and positioned themselves to understand the potential impact on their organizations and communities, found their act of creativity and innovative design to be a competitive advantage over time.

So it is today. Those who find the time to collaborate with each other to identify, understand and develop emerging aspects of the Creative Molecular Economy will find themselves at the cutting edge of change. Deep collaboration will be an important key to the success of a Creative Molecular Economy. For deep collaboration to exist, a new type of ethical behavior based on helping each other succeed is needed.

As an example, a prior General Electric CEO, Jeffery Immelt, emphasized the idea that "Doing Good is Good Business." It was this business mantra that led to GE transforming itself from an Industrial Age behemoth to an adaptable global innovator aligned with the emerging Creative Molecular Economy. Whether developing alternative energies, finding ways to keep the environment sustainable, or insuring ethical and honest behavior for the good of the community, connecting creative people working in collaboration will be a cornerstone of success for communities preparing for a Creative Molecular Economy.

Bringing it Together

Is this the biggest change since the Industrial Revolution? Well, without sticking my neck out too much, I believe so. In fact, I think it may well be the biggest change ever in the economy. It is a deep qualitative change that is bringing intelligent, automatic response to the economy. There's no upper limit to this, no place where it has to end. What I am saying is that it would be easy to underestimate the degree to which this is going to make a difference.
Brian Arthur, *The Second Economy*

The development of any 21st century local economy capable of adapting to constant change will need to "mash-up" individual commitment for learning new capacities for transformation with an emergent culture open to new ideas of any type and attractive to creative people and organizations. Local leaders will have a responsibility to instigate a call to action for cultural change in our communities.

What has not been realized by many of those involved with traditional workforce development initiatives is that in a time of economic and social transformation, concepts and methods must reach beyond reforming traditional practices. Therefore, increasing standard scores in our schools, while helpful, by itself will not prepare students of any age for a different type of economy and society that will be non-linear and require an ability to imagine and to think connectively.

Although improving incentives for industrial and business recruitment will still have some value to employ those who have been displaced, there needs to be a sense of urgency to build an electric infrastructure in parallel able to allow all of its citizens simultaneously to video-stream, to use virtual worlds, and to connect with anyone in the world, without crashing the local system.

It is our hope that organizations and communities dedicated to the creation of a Future Forward Workforce and Creative Molecular Economy will understand the need to rethink their policies and efforts in order to meet individual capacity builder needs of the present at the same time that they work to create a culture able to support a true transformation of thinking and action that is aligned with a very different kind of society and economy that is emerging.

Digitization is creating a second economy that's vast, automatic, and invisible—thereby bringing the biggest change since the Industrial Revolution. Business processes that once took place among human beings are now being executed electronically. They are taking place in an unseen domain that is strictly digital. On the surface, this shift doesn't seem particularly consequential—it's

almost something we take for granted. But I believe it is causing a revolution no less important and dramatic than that of the railroads. It is quietly creating a second economy, a digital one.
Brian Arthur

One of the most important ideas for all local leaders is to recognize that disrutive technologies are transforming our society and communities in ways not understood by most of the citizen leaders in local areas.

In 2012, the Global Risks Report of the Global Economic Forum based in Davos focused on the importance of all societies and local communities to begin to "reconceptualize all of society's institutions" and collaborate together in research and development to be prepared for an Ecological Civilization. This is our call to action. The call to action in this chapter and this book is not an option if we want to have a vital and sustainable society and economy.

Creating Innovation Networks

Sample Strategy Proposal Worksheet

Seeding Community Transformation

Emerging Idea, Weak Signal, Discovery	Potential Impact
Economic: Creating Innovation Networks	Global Innovation Networks will be a key for insuring that local communities have a thriving, entrepreneurial culture.

Strategy For Building Capacities:

1 Recruit chambers and economic development councils to co-sponsor.
2 Recruit an initial group of 5-8 entrepreneurs who would like to develop one or more innovation projects as pilot programs.
3 Identify five emerging ideas, discoveries or inventions to utilize as a key idea.
4 Have 1-2 selected to be the focus for an innovation network.
5 Initiate collaborative processes for those who want to become involved with this new method of economic development.

Expected Outcomes:

1 Individuals use innovation networks to create income streams.

2 Chambers of Commerce become accelerators of innovation networks.

3 Connections are made with entrepreneurs in other areas.

4 Networks of individuals learn how to utilize social networking to find income opportunities.

5 Crowdsourcing becomes a key to innovation networks.

Chapter 5

The Emergence of Polycentric Democracy and Mobile Collaborative Governance

Rethinking Democracy – Developing New Theory and Practice for the Future

We live in a time of great historical disruption and transition where new approaches based on nature's principles of evolution will be the foundation of learning how to adapt quickly to the transformation of our society.

We are reaching the upper limits of representative democracy based on checks and balances. We are on the brink of a true transformation in democratic governance that will exploit the potential of new technologies when combined with new capacities of leaders able to facilitate new processes that can access the opinions and ideas of a broad, diverse, knowledgeable and interested pool of citizens. We need the interest, involvement and knowledge of many people working in collaboration to deal with such complex issues as climate change, reconfiguring global economies, shift of energy systems, biodiversity loss, population growth and the interaction and impacts of multiple new technologies. We call this new form of democracy Polycentric Democracy due to the many different ecosystems of interlocking networks that will emerge as our communities become cauldrons of collaboration and creativity. Eric Liu and Nick Hanauer coined the term Polycentric Democracy in their excellent book, *The Gardens of Democracy*. No longer will we look for the one best answer based on increasingly outdated thinking. We will come together in new ways and build futures projects of research and development.

Many people feel pushed out and disconnected from both their elected leaders and their neighbors. Fewer people are voting, and many of the citizens who do vote elect leaders who are outside of the mainstream and who promise little more than to "shake things up" or "I won't compromise." The good news is that the majority of people say they want to participate in democracy, according to The Harwood Institute, in a study funded by the Kettering Foundation, because they want to have their voices heard. People want their leaders to focus on the best interest of the many not the narrow interest of the privileged. It is imperative that we find better ways to include the public voice in decision making.

It is becoming more obvious that many local leaders are not familiar with trends and weak signals and, as a result, are not able to develop effective strategies for emerging issues. A process we call "mobile connecting" is evolving. With the advent of smart phones and GPS systems, we are entering a new age that will reshape how our society operates by instantaneously accessing the knowledge and opinions of all interested citizens.

This eventually will lead to "Mobile Collaborative Governance," where community leaders, especially in smaller communities, begin to realize that they are not able to keep up with new ideas and methods. These leaders will develop new knowledge connection processes that will utilize community members to identify and facilitate cutting edge concepts and techniques. As these new types of processes develop, a shift will occur from radical individualism, so rampant in our society, to levels of deeper collaboration. In fact, those communities whose leaders become members of larger ecosystems beyond their community boundaries will be able to access intellectual and financial resources to create and test transformational thinking and action in the research and development processes leading to comprehensive community transformation.

Ultimately, a transformational governance and decision making structure will emerge, in our opinion, due to mobile technologies in which as many people in the community as are interested are involved. In his book *The Electronic Republic*, Larry Grossman, former President of NBC News and National Public Radio states *"Technological changes are transforming our political system, creating a new "electronic republic" – a hybrid form that adds elements of direct electronic democracy to America's two-hundred year-old representative republic."*

The age of representative democracy, as we know it, will slowly fade into the dimming glow of Industrial Society. It has served us well, but is too slow to adapt to constantly changing conditions. What is emerging is unknown, but smart mobile technologies, cloud computing and a different kind of leader able to facilitate connections, a Master Capacity Builder, will be key factors in the emerging next phase of democracy ... Polycentric Democracy.

A Natural Evolution

In this time of confusion and disruption due to a level of change that challenges even the best and the brightest to understand what is happening and adapt to constantly changing circumstances, many people see the solution to today's dysfunctional democracy in reclaiming the past. But, trying to find the answers for a different kind of constantly changing future in the ideas and methods of a time of history that looks backward when change evolved slowly, will only lead to frustration and increasing disillusionment.

With that said, it dawned upon us recently that the past, while not holding the answer to a different kind of future, could be helpful in understanding that fundamental principles often provide the basis for a shift in thinking, and that to understand the evolution of key ideas of democracy in the past might very well cause today's leaders to ask fundamental questions for a different kind of age that is in the process of emerging, as did our forefathers.

So we began to explore and read thinkers who have studied

the culture and traditions that birthed our democracy over two hundred years ago. What slowly began to emerge was the idea that new fundamental principles undergirding a 21st century democracy would be required as our society transforms from the Industrial Age to the Organic and Connected Age of an Ecological Civilization.

The Creation of the American Republic by Gordon Wood is one of the books that is helpful in understanding the undergirding ideas of our democracy and how they evolved over time.

One of the chapters in this book is called *Sovereignty of the People*. Three key ideas emerged that reflect an understanding of how to connect fundamental principles of democracy that originated in the past with the transforming needs of democracy for a future of constant change.

According to Wood, the following identifies these three fundamental ideas that undergirded the rise of democracy in the origination of the American Republic over two hundred years ago, and will continue to be important for the future of democracy as long as the "genius and habits" of the people are aligned with the needs of a different type of society that will be more complex, interconnected, real time and fast-paced. In other words, the form of the processes of governance today must conform to the transformation of the society.

Principle #1

Sovereignty of the People

The following quotes from *The Creation of the American Republic* focus on the fundamental idea that power, previously invested in the monarchy and their appointed magistrates, under democratic structures, came from "the people."

Whatever is constituted and ordained by the principle, supreme

power of the people, cannot be altered, suspended or abrogated by
any other power.

Never before had power and decision making rested in everyday people. The Great Experiment of democracy in America had little historical precedent, and was a testimony to the ability of leaders in the late 18th century to challenge not only the power of the British Empire but also the intellectual assumptions of the past, that the "common sense" of average people would give them the ability to govern themselves.

They were, in fact, tending not only to a radical redistribution of the
power of society within government, but to a total destruction of
these powers a shattering of the categories of government that had
dominated Western thinking for centuries.

We are at another juncture of history in which the people must change for the next phase of democracy, Polycentric Democracy, to emerge and function effectively. Not only is there a need to broaden citizen engagement as creative collaborators, a passion for thinking about the future will be required as new knowledge explodes in all areas of society.

As Johnathan Boucher warned, by resting the whole structure of
government on the unmitigated willingness of the people to obey, the
Americans were making a truly revolutionary transformation of
authority.

It is this idea that is being strained due to the need for new ways for citizens to be involved beyond periodic voting for representatives. Although a huge challenge to redesign processes of citizen engagement and decision making, it is no less a challenge that was faced by the forefathers of the 18th century. What seems to be missing is the idea that existed during the American Revolution that leaders need to put themselves and their self-interest behind the common good....and the concomitant good.

The alignment of power with the people and not with the kings was a true transformation of how decisions were to be made that affected the health and security of the populace.

We live in a similar time of transition and transformation in which the next phase of democracy is waiting to be birthed that will be aligned with the "habits of the people". A new framework of parallel processes in which citizen engagement can be self-organizing will be key to the future vitality and sustainability of our society.

It only makes sense that if all individuals can be electronically connected and involved as consumers, entrepreneurs and dating, that the decision making process of governance needs to be re-conceptualized to provide similar methods that can adapt quickly to changing conditions.

Principle #2

Republicanism & The Common Good

One of the greatest misunderstandings in today's democracy is the concept of a republic. When people say we have a republic and not a democracy, it reflects a significant misunderstanding of the fact that the concept of a republic not only relates to how a democracy is structured, but to the emphasis of decision making resting within the body of the public.

The word 'republic,' said Thomas Paine, means the public good, or the good of the whole, in contradiction to the despotic form which makes the good of the sovereign, or one man, the only object of government.

Applying the original Whig (the Whigs were a political party made up of ardent supporters of the Revolution) principle to allow people a maximum voice in the government to the world of today will require the use of cutting edge communication technologies to include virtual reality, a new approach to leadership that designs decision making processes that are aligned with the needs of any local community, and an electorate that is willing to spend time learning about the emergence of weak signals and trends. For any future democracy to be effective will require broadened engagement of diverse people and organizations willing to create and test new ideas and methods appropriate to a constantly changing society that is increasingly complex.

> *Virtue was truly the lifeblood of the republic. The thoughts and hopes surrounding the concept of public spirit gave the revolution a socially radical character – an expected alteration of the very behavior of the people.*

All of the quotes above reflect a set of values important when balancing the needs of the individual with the needs of the community. The character of the people in the late 18th century combined with opportunities for individual liberty not available to traditional European cultures in which power resided in the monarch and aristocracy.

We live in a time no less challenging when individual liberty is often confused with greed and license. As a result of instant communication and transparency not possible in the past, there is an even greater opportunity in the 21st century to bring democracy to the most cherished potential of those dreamers of the Revolution in which the majority of citizens would add value to the society and economy.

It is in the spirit of the potential for the future of our Republic, that we remember the words of Benjamin Franklin when exiting the proceeding of the creation of the Constitution in Philadelphia in 1787. When asked by a lady, "well, Mr Franklin, do we have a republic or a monarchy," he replied, "a Republic if you can keep it."

What values are held to by today's citizenry is key to the response to that question 229 years later. We believe that the majority of citizens, when introduced to the potential of a new approach to democracy in which they can not only vote but also participate as creators of new ideas, methods and processes, will be inspired to collaborate with each other to develop a set of institutional approaches that will align their democracy with the needs of a 21st century society that cannot wait for annual elections and that will require new forms of democratic processes and decision making.

Principle #3

The Forms of Democracy

For every age, there is a form of democracy that must be aligned with the characteristics and structure of the society.

Government takes its form from the genius and habits of the people, and if on paper a form is not accommodated to those habits, it will assume a new form, in spite of all the formal sanctions of the supreme authority of the state.

The above quotes reflect the fact that the originators of our democracy and form of government recognized that major adjustments and new methodologies would need to be created in times of change to take the place of older forms of government that would not be able to adapt quickly to new challenges and requirements that were not predictable when the older form of democracy was created.

We live in such a time when the tension of honoring the past and preparing for a new age exists at all times in different ways. Even the originators of the Constitution recognized that it would need to adapt to future needs not predictable in the late 1800s. Today we need more than amending the Constitution, we need a new framework of decision making that is aligned with the needs of a society that is increasingly fast-paced, interconnected, interdependent and complex.

New ideas about politics were not the product of extended rational analysis, but were rather numerous responses of different Americans to a swiftly changing reality of men involved in endless polemics compelled to contort and draw out from prevailing assumptions the latent logic few had foreseen. Rarely before 1787 were these thoughts comprehended by anyone as a whole. There were bits and pieces thrown up by the necessities of argument and condition, whether broad design or significance. But if crystallized by sufficient pressures they could result in a mosaic of an entirely new conception of politics to those who would attempt to describe it.

The concept of representation was designed to meet the needs of a relatively slowly changing society where power was blunted by the separation of powers and the unique nature of the two representative bodies. Today's fast pace of change overwhelms the capacity of effective response in an age where radical change is increasingly exponential. The new concepts of Polycentric Democracy and Mobile Collaborative Governance will emerge to fit the "genius and habits" of a people who live in a real time reality able to respond instantly and adapt to constantly changing conditions.

... and as was stated over two hundred years ago by the leaders of democratic thinking, the best way of realizing "the public good" in the Whig mind was to allow people a maximum voice in the government.

This is the emerging future genius and habits of interested people involved in real time response and adaptive planning ... Mobile Collaborative Governance.

Turning Democracy's Page

I know of no safe depository of the ultimate powers of the society but the people themselves; and if we think them not enlightened enough to exercise their control with a wholesome discretion, the remedy is not to take it from them but to inform their discretion.

What you need to know about the past is that no matter what happened, it has all worked together to bring you to this very moment. And this is the moment you can choose to make everything new. Right now.

Thomas Jefferson

With this in mind, the following offers a framework of thinking and action to begin to see and build a network of communities interested in collaborating in a research and development effort to create a "21st Century Experiment in Direct Democracy."

Rationale

Contrary to common assumptions, individuals acting collectively have a far greater power to control their circumstances, and indeed of the whole world, than governments pretend. The immediate overthrow of governments now would only bring chaos. But as individuals and groups begin to assert their own agency over decisions and events within their own reach, there will eventually emerge a much wider and more fundamental effect, one that would ultimately amount to a revolution in how we organize our affairs.

Carne Ross

The Leaderless Revolution

With the advent of mobile devices such as smart phones and tablets, a new door has started to open for local governance that, if opened wide over the next decade, will have a major impact on the way democracy operates in a fast-paced, constantly changing society. Over the last thirty years the capacity to govern effectively at the local level has run into four key challenges that the representative system has been unable to resolve effectively:

- The complexity of society has exploded exponentially, straining the capacity of a representative democracy to provide a new kind of citizen engagement, adequate information, and leaders who have the facilitative capacity to think about the future and involve a broader base of citizens in new ways.

- The fundamental principle of the "sovereignty of the people" requires a knowledgeable public. In a time of radical change, a key challenge, as Jefferson so presciently identified, is "to inform their discretion."

- The numbers and quality of those seeking elective office have diminished, while the lack of trust in representative government has increased.

- The resolution of emerging complex issues remains within the context of traditional thinking instead of futures thinking, thus adding to the frustration of democratic decision making.

As a result, the representative system that has served us so well for over two hundred years has reached its own limitation and finds itself unable to adapt quickly enough to the constant change of 21st century society.

With this in mind, we offer a new concept of how our democracy can be redesigned that will take advantage of the knowledge of all interested citizens combining the use of modern communications technology with new leadership processes of citizen facilitation and continuous learning within a futures context.

A quick note. If you believe that democracy as it is currently practiced in the United States is completely resistant to change there are several early prototype experiments in electronic governance and choice making. In 1996, James Fishkin launched a National Issues Convention, which was a deliberative poll broadcast on PBS that allowed ordinary voters to engage Presidential candidates. The Kettering Foundation has televised several of its excellent National Issues Forums from the National Press Club in Washington, DC and of course we can watch CNN host Townhall conversations on critical issues and Presidential races. There are limitations in each of these experiments as television viewers can watch but not engage candidates or vote on issues.

There is also the innovative e-the People.org which has created voter guides that over 13 million people have used across the country. These voter guides have the stamp of approval from the League of Women Voters. A transformative model for local issue deliberation and choice making is the 21st Century Town Meeting created by Carolyn Lukensmeyer in which residents are brought together to dialogue with their neighbors, vote on issues using electronic key pads or their cell phones and have their ideas substantially frame or influence public issues or government policy. 21st Century Town Meetings can be expensive to produce and provide few opportunities for ongoing engagement but they have been used to help decide how to rebuild the Word Trade Center site, New Orleans after Katrina and the city budgets of the District of Columbia. All of these innovations provide important confirmation that people want to be heard more clearly and that there are weak signals indicating interest in new forms of democratic deliberation.

The difference with these methods of citizen input and the Mobile Collaborative Governance idea of Polycentric Democracy is that the citizens are in control of each of the phases of the Direct Consensus Democracy process of Mobile Collaborative Governance....identifying emerging issues and factors relevant to the most important issue, designing appropriate strategies to resolve the issue, and voting directly to select the best strategy. In this way the talent of the entire community of those who want to be involved can be utilized.

The Concept – Mobile Collaborative Governance

The evolution of anticipatory democracy, and the advances and setbacks it has faced over three decades, reinforces the importance of developing shared vision. The more effectively efforts have developed shared vision, particularly across diverse communities, the more successful these efforts have been.
Clem Bezold, *Journal of Futures Studies, November 2010*

The concept of Mobile Collaborative Governance as suggested is an emerging system that integrates process(es) for direct decision making by interested citizens. This emerging system combines project and systemic approaches, individualized, mobile, small communications technologies available for any citizen, knowledge and skills of Master Capacity Builders (able to design and facilitate such a system) and the ability to develop capacities for transformation. Such an approach will enable the general populace to consider emerging issues within a futures context.

Mobile Collaborative Governance will evolve as three parallel processes (any one of which can be utilized separately or together) within the context of Polycentric Democracy:

- As a way for elected officials and staff to access information in real time from interested citizens on existing issues (reforming, not transformational). Put lists into boxes.

1   Establish virtual site for citizens to sign up for their input when requested.
2   Provide app for mobile governance that can be downloaded.
3   Create format for questionnaires.
4   Show results on website that can be accessed.

- As a process to design and implement research and development "futures projects" around emerging issues important to the transformation of local areas.

1   Have site that identifies emerging issues.
2   Provide space for each interested citizen to select issue on which he/she wants to participate.
3   Have form provided that will allow citizen to provide their personal profile to include background, skills, abilities and knowledge areas.
4   Provide virtual facilitators who will be able to help frame any emerging issue within a futures context.
5   Once strategy for emerging issue is defined, develop action plan for a community research and development project.

- As a new platform for a five phase community-based process to:

1   Identify the most important issue(s) for any community annually.
2   Establish a face-to-face and virtual "citizens congress" for

teams to identify key factors important to the number one issue resulting from Phase One. Each team would have a "futures facilitator" able to add key trends, weak signals and transformational factors without manipulating outcome of the group.

3   Each citizen congress team would be given an expected time frame to develop a strategy to resolve the issues based on the multiple factors that had been defined.

4   Representatives from each team (elected by the group) would meet with core facilitators to review all strategies and reduce to a minimum number.

5   Those minimum strategies would be voted on by citizens who sign up using their mobile devices. For those people without a mobile device, a fund will be created that provides access.

21st Century Neighborhood Academies

Until we learn to think differently, there is no reason to act differently, and no reason for our communities to achieve social and economic vitality and sustainability in a constantly changing world.

As with any fundamental shift in thinking, the development of Polycentric Democracy will need time and commitment from dedicated people who are willing to risk moving beyond the comfort of traditional ideas. The gestation stage for the new decision making system of Mobile Collaborative Governance has taken over a decade. Now that the framework of the concept has been identified, it will be important for a network of interested communities to work with the Center for Communities of the Future and collaborating universities to develop pilot programs and find what works and what needs to be adapted and changed as we learn together.

A collaborative network of communities in different states of the U.S. and provinces in Canada is in the early stage of developing the foundational phase of futures learning so important to the potential success of Mobile Collaborative Governance.

The first step of this occurred in July, 2015, when representatives from Chestermere, Canada; Livermore, California; and Manhattan, Kansas, introduced the idea of "21st century neighborhood academies" at the World Future Society Conference in San Francisco.

Each colleague has committed to developing a network of core groups in different neighborhoods to seed and evolve knowledge about emerging weak signals and trends. Below is the framework of a concept for "21st century neighborhood academies" to be seeded and developed in Manhattan, Kansas over the next several years. Dr. Mike Ribble of the Manhattan Public Schools and author of Digital Citizenship designed this version that will be appropriate for their community.

Below is all of the information we gave potential participants in the program that explains how the a 21st Century Neighborhood Academy works, and what the benefits are for a community.

What is a 21st Century Neighborhood Academy?

A 21st Century Neighborhood Academy is an idea that is emerging from dialogue among the Center for Communities of the Future (COTF) and other groups throughout the country to prepare local neighborhoods for a different kind of society that will evolve in the first half of this century. 21st Century Neighborhood Academies will emphasize the needs of the present and those of the future in parallel processes. The processes, methods and concepts of the Center for Communities of the Future and other groups will be integrated to help neighborhoods focus on both short-term needs in parallel to the need to build "capacities for transformation" for a constantly changing and more complex society.

A key emphasis of each 21st Century Neighborhood Academy will be to help interested residents recognize the need to learn how to become comfortable with transformative change and the uncertainty that is a product of such change. The principle of transformation undergirds the concept and practice of 21st Century Neighborhood Academies.

The most fundamental assumptions of our society are being challenged. The residents of all neighborhoods will need to understand how trends will impact their individual lives, their families, and their communities. How residents respond to these challenges will determine whether they and their neighborhoods will be vital and sustainable.

21st Century Neighborhood Academies are safe havens where interested residents are able to come together to:

- Learn what are important future trends.
- Understand the impact of trends on themselves and their neighborhoods.
- Identify key issues important to the neighborhood within a "future context."
- Develop "capacities for transformation" that will help residents prepare for constant change.
- Design and implement "21st century projects" which will prepare the neighborhood for the future.
- Learn how to network with human, financial and technical resources anywhere in the world in support of neighborhood activity.

21st Century Neighborhood Academies build the capacities of neighborhoods and individuals to engage in "transformative change" by introducing the participants to new concepts such as transformational thinking, transformational learning, and transformational action.

Why Are 21st Century Neighborhood Academies Needed?

21st Century Neighborhood Academies are needed to prepare residents to think differently, to learn how to collaborate at a deeper level, and to develop 21st century capacities not present in the existing neighborhood.

There will be an increasing need to develop parallel efforts in local neighborhoods that take care of existing problems (safety, pot holes in streets, beautification, etc.) at the same time that interested residents are introduced to concepts of futures thinking not traditionally seen as important.

Whether preparing residents to participate in a Creative Molecular Economy, building future basic skills or helping them become a learning community, 21st Century Neighborhood Academies are designed to integrate a context of futures thinking in the consciousness of a core group of neighborhood leaders. Any neighborhood needs to have at least ten percent of its resident body become familiar with future trends and begin to understand how to anticipate the impact of these trends on their neighborhoods ... and to share with other neighbors.

How Would a 21st Century Academy Work for My Neighborhood?

21st Century Neighborhood Academies have the following framework:

- Groups of 8 to 15 neighborhood residents are recruited/ volunteer to participate.
- Those that become involved receive incentives: Community cash that can be utilized with local sponsors of each project.
  - Free books and other material important to the

academy.

- ○ Free access to a computer connected to the Internet.
- ○ A free computer for those that finish the neighborhood academy.
- ○ Introduction to co-sponsoring organizations and businesses for better jobs.
- ○ Potential mentors who would support continued development of the skills introduced in the 21st Century Academy.
- Master Capcity Builders are coached by the Center for Communities of the Future.
- Three ring 21st Century Academy binders are provided for each participant.
- Bi-weekly sessions are held in a home or neighborhood facility.
- Each 21st Century Academy is tailored for the level of interest and needs of the neighborhood. It is expected that all participants will commit to attend all meetings and work with the material. Therefore, only those that have real interest should be initially involved.
- It is understood that this effort is parallel and complementary to existing neighborhood projects and is focused on developing capacities for transformation over the longer term.

Why Should Neighborhood Residents Become Involved?

Participation in 21st Century Academies develops the abilities, knowledge, and skills to engage in "transformative change" with the following results:

- Improved abilities of individuals to understand, participate and lead in an environment of change.
- Increased ability of the neighborhood to see a need to work

together because of the more complex nature of future issues.

- An ability of generations to understand each other's point of view.
- Increased 21st century thinking and technology skills leading to improved income opportunities as the economy begins to emphasize the development of electronic entrepreneurs capable of innovative thinking.
- Interpersonal skills based on new ways of thinking which lead to less conflict and new ways of collaboration.
- The ability to utilize new innovative ideas for emerging neighborhood needs.

What Outcomes Can Be Expected From 21st Century Academies?

Each 21st Century Academy is tailored to the needs of the neighborhood to insure the following outcomes:

- An increased understanding of how future trends interact in ways that would not be anticipated.
- An ability to see connections among diverse factors and ideas leading to innovations for individuals, families and the neighborhood.
- An ability for "collaboratives" to understand how to develop comprehensive, transformative strategies to resolve existing issues and anticipated challenges.
- A reduction in neighborhood conflict as participants are taught how to find value in the other person's point of view.
- The use of futures thinking to help diverse people learn how to connect their knowledge and background with others in an act of creation to help their neighborhood prepare for change.
- Develop a small group of "master capacity builders" in

each neighborhood able to expand resident networks capable of 21st century thinking and action.

- Develop the ability to identify key issues and access the potential for transformation existing in each neighborhood.

These 21st Century Academies can add immense value to the potential of neighborhood residents in order to prepare them for the increasing demands of an interconnected and increasingly fast-paced society and economy. Of special interest is the fact that the participants in their jobs, their families, their leisure time activities and their involvement as citizens can utilize the capacities developed in each academy.

Why is Transformation a Key Concept for Each 21st Century Academy?

All citizens are faced with the need to understand that work in the future will be increasingly mental and less physical. In addition, knowledge will continue to explode leaving those behind who do not have a core base of knowledge about future trends and their impact.

In addition, additional skills will be needed to help the residents of all neighborhoods become productive citizens:

- The ability to see connections using and/both thinking.
- The ability to ask appropriate questions.
- The ability to listen at a deeper level in order to see value in what the other person is saying.
- The ability to anticipate weak signals before they become trends.
- The ability to create innovations base on transformative thinking.
- The ability to know how to learn more than facts and content of knowledge, the ability to see more than one

thing at a time.

We live in a time of apparent contradictions. When we try to make what we have always done more efficient, things often seem to get worse. At the same time, completely new technologies and ways of thinking are creating an explosion of possibilities to transform how we work, learn and make decisions. Consider the following:

- The world grows smaller and more connected, both technologically and systemically leading to increased complexity and real time stresses ... especially for those less skilled and unable to think in new ways.
- The phrase "24/7" becomes a commonplace description of how we function often leaving no time for relationships.
- Public and private sector institutions and neighborhoods are often dysfunctional and not able to work in collaboration to solve problems and develop new ideas.
- Businesses operate in an increasingly unpredictable environment that grows more competitive on a daily basis often without an ethical and moral compass which will support healthy societies.
- All people are in a time crunch, stressed, and more disengaged from community, work and each other.
- Our physical and human environments are increasingly at risk.

Reprising Mobile Collaborative Governance

If anyone doubts the growth of civil discord that has the potential for overwhelming today's society, consider the lack of respect among competing parties throughout the country, the expanding frustration of the middle class, the increasing on the ground demonstrations of citizens again the misuse of wealth and power, and the near total inability of political parties to find common ground on anything.

In addition, the media increasingly stokes the fires of discord and distrust to increase ratings. Talking heads often introduce leading questions to their guests that border on bullying rather than having an open, civil dialogue among people with different points of view.

When the President addresses the nation in the State of the Union, the opposing party immediately responds in a way that often goes beyond introducing a different point of view. Today we see speeches (some bordering on rants) in both houses of Congress broadcast live on C-Span, but often no one appears to be in attendance. This is not effective discourse that leads to good public policy, but, unfortunately, the experience of governance that lately we have come to expect.

It is as if we have reverted to the time of the ancient Roman Senate when Roman satirist Juvenal (cir 100 AD), made the observation:

The people long eagerly for two things; bread and circuses.

In a recent conversation with a local congressman, the question was asked whether the business of the people could be handled effectively with no time to talk, and even less time to consider the emerging complexity of life and political challenges. He argued that in the old days before affordable commercial airlines, members of congress were forced to be more civil. Such a comment reflects a drastic change in the American culture, and that the principles and ethics of those who are now called the greatest generation were not forced to work together, but worked together to utilize their differences effectively because of the values that were just as concerned about the society as their self-interest. The point was made that American politics has always been rough and tumble, but that there is a current existing in our present political discourse in which only those speaking have the truth, and that the ends justifies the means to be re-elected. The very nature of civility is being squeezed from the body politic, and needs to be restored as if the ghosts of Sam Ervin, Ronald Regan, and Daniel (Pat) Moynihan have returned to remind us of the roles and responsibilities of representatives who embody the sovereignty of the people.

Yes, it is true that during the past, representatives usually lived in the same areas of the District of Columbia and often had meals together without regard to party. They actually communicated rather than ranting at each other through the media.

Today, too often, our elected leaders have become ideologues, and extremists; both sides are guilty. There is little to no real dialogue and effective interaction with each other or their electorate that leads to a consensus of new ideas appropriate for a constantly changing society. At best, town hall meetings are held so that elected officials can extol the virtue of "consulting my constituents." Theses venues seem to serve more as a political stump and supporter rally than true dialogue. A perversion of the democratic process and society is reflected in the perceived need of some citizens to carry concealed weapons. Even with a law enforcement presence there is still fear because of the shift of emphasis to the often irrational views of extremists on all sides of the political spectrum. The pendulum no longer swings between different ideas of what is effective political thinking. The pendulum of balance has broken off at the pivot because of the inability and unwillingness of those in positions of power to see value in other points of view. Added to this is the danger of many of those in power not caring about discerning emerging truths as a part of a newly developing society ... but only caring about their perception of truth based on looking at the past for guidance. It seems the only voice with influence is those of special interest groups and political action committees ... and these groups by definition want to maintain the status quo and the inherent, existing power.

Most unfortunate is the too often shared belief that this is how all levels of government operate. The rancor and political disconnect portrayed in the national media unfortunately is seen as infusing its virus in those involved with local government. In fact it is not true. Local elected leaders and their staff are the most connected to the citizen. They attend church with them, their children go to the same schools, and they pay the same taxes and utility bills. Local elected officials rarely connect with members of Congress or their state legislature. However, many citizens assume otherwise and see politicians at all levels as corrupt, only out to influence decisions to benefit themselves or their associates. It has been termed as the "congressionalization" of the country. Most papers written on this identify "congressional-ization" with lobbyists and professional consultants involved with polling and political strategy. I submit that too often citizen perception of congressionalization extends beyond this limited academic view, leading to a generalization that all government is bad and "us" against "them."

One emerging idea that we feel has the potential to reverse this trend, or at least to allow people to have the opportunity to become involved with local decisions at different levels is the concept of Mobile Collaborative Governance. This new concept of Mobile Collaborative Governance offers the opportunity for any citizen to be more connected to one's elected official and, more importantly, to participate directly when appropriate in the decision making process.

Mobile Collaborative Governance has the great potential of moving beyond the era of special interest and the effect of lobbyists. I often tell my council they should make routine visits to the state capitol and to the District of Columbia. Just as our elected officials need to see the local elected officials and hear their concerns, there is a need for a new system of citizen partic-ipation that not only allows local officials to know of their concerns, but also allows citizens to feel that their opinion and voice will make a difference ... our democracy has come to a point where that is not the case generally today.

Whether it is commenting on policy using a Twitter account to alert citizens of ribbon cuttings announcing new businesses moving into the area, the use of communications technology to warn people of pending natural disaster, or, even more important in the long run, to work in collaboration to develop ideas and design projects to help any local community prepare for a different kind of economy and society, the potential of Mobile Collaborative Governance to recapture civility in our society is huge.

As mayors and other elected officials begin to understand the potential and see the value of Mobile Collaborative Governance, they will want to involve as many citizens as possible, especially the youth. Very few students know who the mayor and council members are, much less about what they do. Many students do not understand the connection of elected officials even though they drive to a school built and managed with local dollars, on streets paved with local funds, drink water, and use electricity ... all provided by the local government.

Rethinking the established system with a new concept of governance that is aligned with the needs of a newly emerging society and economy that is interdependent and constantly changing will return sovereignty to the people and reenergize our political system.

We live in a time when new ideas and needs are converging to transform every aspect of our society. In a time when newly emerging communication technologies create instantaneous, real time flow of information, our democracy must have civility for it to survive and thrive. Without civility, issues will remain polarized, and citizens will reduce increasingly complex problems into black and white traditional thinking because it is convenient and easier to do without learning new knowledge and skills. Public dialogue at any time is not an easy process.

However, a future based on different principles and concepts will need a new type of dialogue ... a "futures generative dialogue." Mobile Collaborative Governance will tap the "wisdom of the people" in a new way to build "capacities for transformation" for a society increasingly fast-paced, interconnected and complex. And, in so doing, will, at long last, help our democracy reach its full potential.

Mobile Collaborative Governance

Sample Strategy Proposal Worksheet

Seeding Community Transformation

Emerging Idea, Weak Signal, Discovery	Potential Impact
Governance: Community Futures Generative Dialogue (FGD) Rooms	Establishing "generative dialogue" rooms throughout a community will become a magnet for those people who want to prepare for a different kind of future.

Strategy For Building Capacities:

1 Participating Individuals are introduced to the concept of weak signals.
2 Weak signals identified can be shared with other community groups.
3 Over time, a culture open to new ideas supporting continuous innovation is created.
4 Transformational ideas will emerge and pilot projects spun off.
5 A community network of citizens will be able to deal with emerging issues within a "futures context."

Expected Outcomes:

1 Involve the central library and branches to hold monthly

FGD sessions.

2 Promote the project on-line and in the local press.

3 Coach facilitators in how to introduce weak signals for a group dialogue.

4 Give those who participate a list of books, articles and websites to be used for identifying emerging ideas, discoveries and inventions.

5 Have the results of the monthly sessions put on a community website to involve citizens in transformational projects that are spun off from the dialogue.

Chapter 6

pH Ecosystem: A Comprehensive Approach to Community-Based Preventive Healthcare

Let's take a look at one particular part of the "comprehensive community transformation" ecosystem that focuses on a comprehensive approach to healthcare. This is an example of a "transformational concept" in that it shifts emphasis from intervention to a community-based approach to prevention.

As you read this chapter, consider how many of the previous ideas and methods are found in this new approach to healthcare for local areas.

The intent of this chapter is to provide a specific example or concept paper for how transformational thinking and action can be introduced and implemented in any community.

The Theory of Healthcare and Complex Adaptive Systems (Dr.Paul Laurienti)

During the past centuries, the goal of healthcare to help individuals live their lives as long as possible and as healthy as possible has remained relatively unchanged.

Most Americans are familiar with the healthcare system – the hospitals, doctors, nurses, and others we turn to when we are sick or hurt.

However, the challenges facing those in the healthcare industry have changed.

Western medicine is masterful at achieving the first objective of healthcare – keep people alive as long as possible. Western medicine excels at treating acute disease. If you have community acquired pneumonia, western medicine will cure you. The massive amount of biomedical research that has been performed, particularly in the United States, is a major reason western medicine is so good at treating acute disease.

Biomedical research is based on reductionist scientific thinking. Break a system down into individual parts, study and understand those parts, and put the system back together to understand how it functions. This methodology is excellent for acute disease, primarily because an acute illness is focused in a restricted part of the system (body). An acute bout of pneumonia in an otherwise healthy person is an infection that is localized to the lungs. The disease does not affect the entire system.

Keeping people healthy in later life was not a challenge in 1900 when the life expectancy was below 50 years old. The challenge in 1900 was keeping people alive, not keeping them healthy.

In 2010, the life expectancy at birth in the U.S. was 78.7 years old. However, as we live longer we are also experiencing more chronic disease associated with natural degeneration. Additionally, changes in our environment and society have resulted in changes in our general health, e.g., increasing rates of heart disease, hypertension, diabetes, and depression.

In fact experts suggest that 60% of overall health is determined by social, economic, and environmental factors.

Many factors are associated with lifestyle choices. For example, our diets changed, our physical activity changed, our habits (smoking, alcohol use, etc.) changed. Health is also determined in large part by access to social and economic opportunities, the resources and supports available in our homes, neighborhoods, and communities; the quality of our schooling; the safety of our workplaces; the cleanliness of our water, food, and air; and sense of community we find as the result of our social interactions and relationships. Health is deeply rooted in all aspects of our lives and how we live each day.

All of these factors, together, have resulted in a massive change in our healthcare needs. We transitioned from needing urgent healthcare to keep us alive to needing long-term healthcare and an emphasis on wellness that will allow us to live healthy lives.

Of additional concern is the knowledge that healthcare has become an increasingly expensive and unsustainable proposition. Total healthcare spending in the United States is estimated to be $8895 per capita ($5741 per capita in Canada).

The Organization for Economic Co-operation and Development (OECD) gathers statistics concerning heath and disease in its 34 member countries across the world. A recent article in the *Journal of The American Medical Association* evaluated the U.S. healthcare system from 1990-2010. This enlightening article shows that approximately one half of the U.S. healthcare burden in 2010 was associated with chronic disease. In addition, according to most measures of health, the U.S. declined in ranking over this 20-year period compared to the other 34 countries. This occurred while the U.S. spent more on healthcare than any other country. In fact, the U.S. spent over 17% of the gross domestic product (GDP) on healthcare in 2010. The next nearest country was the Netherlands at 12.1%. Based on calculations using The World Bank data, the U.S. far exceeded any other country in raw dollars by spending 2.6 trillion dollars. The next closest county was Japan at 500 billion dollars.

So, the obvious question is – Why is health in the U.S. declining (relative to other nations) despite exorbitant expenditures on healthcare and the largest biomedical research budget in the world? A more proactive question is – how can we use our abundant resources to improve individual health and wellness as well as our capacities for resiliency? Now is the time to shift our perspective and retarget our resources in healthcare delivery and biomedical research. These very methods and conceptual frameworks that have yielded so much success in understanding and treating acute disease are failing us in chronic disease.

There are many possible explanations. Yet it is undeniable – chronic disease is a systemic problem. Each part of the body is influenced by a chronic disease via direct and indirect routes and to greater or lesser extents. The human body is a complex adaptive system (CAS). It is made up of interacting sub-systems, each made up of interacting parts. In a CAS, changes in one part may cascade and alter virtually any other part of the system.

Before discussing how CAS and systems thinking can benefit healthcare and biomedical research, it is important to re-define a CAS. We have discussed this previously in the book and this is a living example.

Consider a murmuration (flock) of starlings as they fly through the sky. This system is composed of hundreds or thousands of individual birds. However, the birds function together, producing amazing flocking behaviors not dictated by a central controller. Each bird does what it chooses. There is no individual orchestrating the flock. Yet, the birds fly in concert and they do it as if all dance as a single entity. The apparent unified behavior of a murmuration of starlings is an emergent property of the system.

Scott E Page from the University of Michigan provides us with a definition of a CAS. According to Page, a CAS is a system where the individual components have four main properties.

First, the individual components are interconnected. They form networks in which each component has some connection or relationship to other components. In the murmuration of starlings, each bird has neighboring birds that it can see, hear, and feel.

Second, they are interdependent. It is not enough to be connected; the components must influence each other. When starlings are flocking, the flight pattern of each bird is highly dependent on the fight patterns of nearby birds.

Third, the components that make up the system must be diverse. This diversity is often expressed in variable response thresholds. So while a murmuration only contains starlings, each bird will respond to the behaviors of other birds with a different sensitivity.

Finally, the components must be able to adapt. They must change over time and this change is the result of the interactions they have with the other parts of the system. A starling flying in a flock must continuously change its speed, direction, altitude, and its sensitivity in response to the behavior of others.

A living organism is a self-organized CAS (complex adaptive system) with all its parts interacting. The whole bears no resemblance in shape or function to its individual parts. The individual parts cannot exhibit the same behaviors as the whole system. The flock of starlings does not look or act like an individual bird, and the individual starling cannot produce flocking behavior.

The human body is a complex system consisting of trillions of diverse cells all working in concert. Chronic disease is an alteration of the functional coordination between the individual parts of the human body. This dysfunction can result in dramatic changes in biochemistry, physiology, and anatomy.

Obesity is an excellent example of a systemic health problem where the accumulation of fat changes the structure and function of virtually every part of the body. Just last year (2013) the American Medical Association recognized obesity as a disease. It is well known that obesity is a risk factor for a large number of other diseases including, but not limited to, diabetes, heart disease, liver disease, physical disability, cancer, and even cognitive decline. How is it that accumulations of fat can be related to so many other disorders? Fat not only directly alters the mechanical properties of bones, joints, and muscles through changes in weight, but fat cells are metabolically active, release many chemical messengers, and are in turn affected by chemical and physical signals from other systems.

Obesity is a complex disease that alters virtually every other sub-system in the body and is the result of the interactions between many factors. The reductionist prescription to decrease food intake and increase exercise has not successfully alleviated the obesity epidemic that our nation currently faces. No one argues that decreased caloric intake and increased caloric expenditure will result in weight loss, yet such a behavior change is incredibly complex. Many factors must be considered. There is no singular solution for obesity. Many factors including biochemical, physiological, environmental, genetic, social, economic, and cognition must be considered.

Eating behavior is highly complex in its own right. Not only do we eat to acquire nutrients, but we also eat out of desire, for comfort, for pleasure, and as a coping mechanism. The human brain is integral in controlling our eating behavior and the body can modulate brain activity associated with eating. Recent research has demonstrated that brain networks in older overweight adults are highly sensitive to food restriction. It has also shown and that various traits, such as the ability to resist food in an obesogentic environment, are associated with particular brain connectivity patterns. Understanding an individual's brain connectivity patterns may be useful for designing personalized weight loss interventions that can facilitate successful behavioral change.

Eating behavior is not only modulated by our brain physiology, it is a highly social activity. Social factors are major contributors to health. A study in 2007 clearly demonstrated that obesity can spread through social networks. The finding was alarmingly strong. Over a period of time, a person was 57% more likely to become obese if a friend became obese during that period. The underlying mechanism for this spread is not fully understood. It is likely that social norms contribute as well as our tendency to judge ourselves according to our peers.

Economic status is also a highly relevant issue. The foods that an individual can afford can have significant effects on metabolism and weight. It is generally accepted that the healthiest calories are those obtained from unprocessed foods, particularly fruits and vegetables. These fresh foods are typically more expensive. Buying in bulk can save money, but fresh foods spoil faster. The solution for economically challenged individuals is to buy cheaper foods that will last longer. These typically are processed, calorie-dense foods. Furthermore, the food industries market and promote the purchase and consumption of large portions of calorie dense foods at low prices.

The community and our social networks have a major influence over our physical activity. Living in cities that are highly conducive to walking can promote increased physical activity. Our population is highly concentrated in the suburbs of cities. Due to zoning and neighborhood development, the suburbs are often not designed to promote walking. When a grocery store is located a few blocks from home a person is more likely to walk to the store. However, in many neighborhoods the zoning prohibits small business from being located in the same area as homes. This results in concentrated housing areas miles from concentrated business areas. This neighborhood organization promotes the use of automobiles rather than walking. Increasing biking lanes might promote the use of bicycles in these circumstances. While it is clear that social-economic factors are associated with obesity, similar factors may also serve as a mechanism to spread health through peer-support, spiritually-based organizations, and community health programs.

The behavior changes necessary to reduce obesity are very difficult to realize. A concerted effort is needed to promote healthy lifestyles in an affordable manner. In addition to these social, cognitive, and economic factors, it is important to understand the role of biology in weight gain and weight loss. The caloric content of food used to be determined by burning the food. Today the caloric content of food is calculated based on predetermined values of individual food components (proteins, fats, etc.). These predetermined values are based on burning the particular components. The human body does not burn food, it metabolizes food. This requires a host of enzymes, cofactors, and a lot of biochemistry. Different foods with many different components could all interact in the digestive system and simple calorie counting can be highly misleading. Support for this idea comes from recent studies showing relationships between metabolic disturbances and the ingestion of high fructose corn syrup in humans. The amount of food or calories one ingests is very important, but the specific food can also play a vital role, even when matched for calories.

Recently, the bacterial flora of our gastrointestinal tract has been associated with obesity. Several studies in mice have found specific bacteria in the GI tract can be associated with the development of obesity. Transplanting gut bacteria from obese humans into mice altered the metabolism in the mice and increased body mass and fat. Gut bacteria may be related to obesity because they contribute to our digestive process. They are not just passive inhabitants. While research findings in rodents may not be directly applicable to humans, these studies highlight the complexity within the digestive system. There is growing evidence showing that even in humans, the bacteria in the GI tract can modulate our biochemistry, immune systems, and even influence brain function. Studies show that the diversity of our bacterial flora is decreasing. This has been attributed, as least in part, to use of antibacterial compounds found in soaps and hand sanitizers.

Despite the complexity of chronic diseases, such as the example of obesity provided above, the mainstay of western medicine is to identify a drug that can be used as a treatment. While beyond the scope of this article, much of the focus on finding drugs to manage chronic disease is driven by the business models of the pharmaceutical industry.

Although medicine in western culture is focused on the use of drugs to cure a disease that already exists, other cultures emphasize the prevention of disease through meditation, channeling of energy through the seven chakras, and the use of alternative diets and vitamins.

For obesity, the current hot topic is the development of vaccines. Drugs and vaccines are highly effective for the treatment and prevention of acute disorders. However, in a complex process it is likely ineffective to target a single causative factor when the disorder is an emergent result of many inter-acting factors. This is not to say that one cannot find leverage points in a CAS (complex adaptive system).

Leverage points are parts of a system that when changed have widespread effects throughout the system. Often, the leverage points are not the obvious target. Trying to change the obvious (like reducing food intake and increasing physical activity) can be disappointingly ineffective. Not only that, when manipu-lating a CAS, unintended outcomes often result that are not predictable and are often catastrophic. Adverse side effects from medications are classic examples of such consequences.

Complex Adaptive Systems provides a transformational approach that is non-linear and uses parallel processes. The concept of "and/both" is fundamental to any community-based healthcare approach.

A first step in managing health from a CAS perspective is to recognize that a chronic disease does not have a single cause. This is a major mindset shift. If there is no one cause, then there is no reason to search for the one receptor, one chemical, one hormone, or one gene that is responsible. Rather, one should seek to understand the system and the interactions within the system. It is important that we not only consider multi-faceted approaches but that we look beyond our traditional under-standing of the system. To what degree is the biome contributing to obesity? Are we spreading bacteria throughout our population that are pro-obesogenic? As we isolate components of food and engineer new foods are we missing key ingredients that contribute to health? And, as we learn more about the impact of the social determinants of health, what can we do to reduce the contribution of social, economic, and environmental factors and strengthen our capacities for resiliency?

We have introduced the concept of resiliency in Chapter 4 on the emergence of a Creative Molecular Economy. The ability to adapt to different conditions influenced by the impact of multiple factors is central to the idea of building capacities for comprehensive community transformation whether related to a community-based approach to preventive healthcare or developing interlocking networks of 21st century entrepreneurs.

Currently more than one third of American adults is obese and this number is increasing annually. This is occurring despite ongoing efforts to improve health in our nation. Of course, currently there is no solution for obesity, nor is it commonly believed there is one answer.

All of the factors discussed above, and many more, are contributors. While the extent to which each contributes in a single person likely varies widely across the population, our future is dependent on finding a solution to this problem.

It is expected that the solution to obesity will actually be a system of solutions that all interact and complement each other. Each solution applied in isolation will likely fail. Only when appropriate combinations of solutions are identified and personalized will the individual solutions work to facilitate one another. When the solutions are enacted on a larger scale through lifestyle and community changes we may be able to prevent further obesity.

In a CAS, dysfunction is due to either an external influence (such as an infection) or altered interactions among the elements (chronic disease). Solutions for external influences are simple. Remove the offending agent. Solutions for internal alterations require systems thinking. For chronic disease, the goal should be prevention so we never have to find a cure. If we can prevent the disease we can prevent the need for medicine. If we are unable to prevent the disease, then we must use multi-faceted, systems approaches rather than searching for single-factor solutions such as a pill or a vaccine.

Practical Applications: a Transformational Community-Based Framework (Brenda Herchmer and Jerry Hopkins)

As mentioned throughout the book, the skills and knowledge needed for futures thinking and action need to be seeded and spread throughout any community.

Core groups of transformational leaders who we call Master Capacity Builders need to be developed in order to be able to design and facilitate capacities for transformation using the principles of Complex Adaptive Systems.

To build capacities for transformation of our healthcare system at the local level requires a newly conceived system of healthcare based on the principles of CAS. The concept of resiliency for individuals and communities, the ability to adapt quickly to changing conditions, will be important in an emerging and increasingly fast-paced, interconnected and complex world.

When we begin to view healthcare in this way, the more we see that even programs focused on encouraging individuals to eat healthy, get physically active, and quit smoking will not be enough to bring about health and wellness across an entire community. Complex community issues e.g., homelessness, poverty, poor nutrition, addiction, environmental pollution, isolation etc. will also need to addressed as they also impact health.

As a result, it becomes clear that health and wellness is everyone's responsibility – government at all levels, individuals, families, communities, service providers, non-profit organizations, elected officials, and business and industry will all need to play a role if healthcare is to move in a new direction.

The future of healthcare must shift from an emphasis on intervention to a preventive treatment and care system that reduces the impact of social, economic, and environmental factors and strengthens community resiliency by including the following elements. There needs to be leadership at both the "grasstops" and "grassroots" of our communities that emphasizes the leadership and community building required for comprehensive community transformation. Interlocking collaborative networks of active and engaged citizens involved in knowledge building and prevention activities, as well as treatment and care and a network of 21st century neighborhood academies instilling futures/transformational thinking, integrated delivery systems.

Our communities need to take action by promoting greater system dialogue and response to emerging issues and leading practices by establishing local and regional health and community integration networks and webs that will encourage "meshwork" by supporting state and national dialogue, knowledge transfer, provision of a collective voice, quality, and sustainability. Futures oriented activities, projects and programs involving citizens in fun and engaging ways (being healthy does not have to be an arduous task) can take place at the local level. "Physical and virtual centerpiece" for healthcare prevention and treatment; that is Holarchial in nature to encourage local leaders and citizens to shift into a new paradigm of thinking about healthcare, moving beyond traditional approaches.

The application of the above elements will evolve existing community healthcare components into a Preventive Health Care Ecosystem Holarchy – to be referred to as "pH Ecosystem." Its formation will encourage local leaders and citizens to shift into a new paradigm of thinking about healthcare, and move beyond traditional approaches.

The components (holons) of this Holarchy are the following:

- a pH Ecosystem Collaborative whose members are community residents, healthcare providers (individuals and institutional), governmental agencies concerned about health and wellness, fitness and wellness providers (individuals and institutional), educational institutions (training and research), healthcare payers (public and private), and others that commit to the goal of the pH Cooperative;

- a pH Ecosystem Collaborative Council composed of representatives from interested organizations of the community to develop, manage and operate the pH Ecosystem;

- a pH Ecosystem Center which is an existing community hospital and/or major medical facility in a community which evolves and transforms itself into a coordinating center for community-based prevention – or "health-spital," (Dr. Frank Maletz, Surgeon, East Lyme, CT) to recognize and to connote that effective healthcare in local communities connects intervention and prevention into a holistic system with all parts interdependent and connected; and

- a cadre of pH Ecosystem Paramedics (Dr. Michael Manning), a new type of practitioner who works alongside doctors, nurse practitioners and physician assistants to deliver patient-centered medical care, subsequently referred to as "pH Paramedic."

The pH Ecosystem Collaborative (Dr. Frank Maletz)

One of the key ideas mentioned previously in the book is the need to provide places where people can come together to dream about the future and spin off futures projects using "futures generative dialogue." This is an example of a new approach to being practical in that old ideas are increasingly out of date and ineffective.

We suggest that all communities create "futures stations" where collaborative groups of diverse people come together to think about the future beyond the norm. Such an idea is the concept of a "pH (preventive healthcare) Ecosystem Collaborative" whose participants not only come from various community agencies in the local area, but who also are connected to experts and professionals throughout the world.

The primary responsibility of membership in the pH Ecosystem Collaborative requires a commitment to holistic health with an emphasis on wellness and prevention. Other general responsibilities include a willingness of members to participate in shaping the pH Ecosystem through participation in specific study and work groups, sharing of knowledge, and evaluating transformational innovations from their particular perspective.

Below is a list of the potential elemental drivers of this pH Collaborative:

- **All** persons are included – community wide. The pH Collaborative will focus on universal capture and constant coverage, not just coverage when health or wellness related questions or crises arise; thus, creating dynamic funnelization to **8 Rights**

  Right patient.
  Right provider and provider experience.
  Right place or point of care.
  Right price point.
  Right amount.
  Right diagnosis.
  Right timing.
  Right care.

- Population health and complicated chronic conditions must be managed, care coordinated and integrated.

- Use of functional electronic health records and applications to enable data to be interactive, fungible, and portable.
- Compliance – Data must be interactive, fungible and portable.
- Health gateways into which the above individual health information can be monitored through sophisticated algorithms offering the resident member and/or health provider certain suggestions for prevention, intervention, treatment, or further information collection.
- Death as Life – community respect for the last wishes of the dying, the sick elderly, and the terminally incurables with honor, dignity and respect. Including Hospice as a key cooperative member will be critical to this driver.
- Develop a culture and ethic within the pH Collaborative that focuses upon the reduction of waste, of fraud, of abuse, of unnecessary superfluous redundancies, and of duplication of testing and treatment.
- Availability of sensor equipment within one's home or workplace. Equipment such as weight scales, blood pressure, blood testing, etc. will be connected through tele-health or smart phone applications that transmit the information to data centers where electronic monitoring occurs with practitioners alerted to any deviation from the norm.
- All community members are given a battery of screening questions and tests to determine current baseline of health and potential illnesses.
- All community members are eligible to receive a whole genome screening. The mapping of the individual genome can determine predispositions to certain diseases and certain developmental health issues that may arise in the future. When done as a part of a community, the genomes maps may suggest priority areas for the focus of

prevention.

- Develop a system which shares the economic benefits of cost savings derived from the implementation of the pH Ecosystem to reduce costs of healthcare coverage for resident members or to underwrite the cost of preventive approaches and research.

Certain tools available to resident members will provide the pH Collaborative with a baseline of data, the ability to identify chronic conditions and their potential occurrence more easily, and the information necessary to measure the progress and success of the pH Ecosystem. Every member will have access to and will be encouraged to avail themselves of the following tools.

Functional and interactive digital health records are the first tool. Each individual will be encouraged and assisted (if needed) to complete an electronic profile and health history. These health records will require true portability and connectivity not only with health providers' systems but with social media health applications, tele-health monitors, and health gateways into which this individual health information can be monitored through sophisticated algorithms offering the resident member and/or health provider certain suggestions for prevention, intervention, treatment, or further information collection. The availability of this potential health to pH Collaborative resident members can lead to empowerment in their own prevention and/or care efforts.

All pH Collaborative resident members are given access to the preventive and wellness measures developed by the pH Collaborative, to treatment as may be required, and to other care as needed. Subgroups of resident members such as the frail elderly and individuals with disabilities may require added access to specific types of care such as home care, personal care, dementia care, etc.

All other pH Collaborative members will work together to

deliver the preventive, wellness, intervention, treatment, and care services required by the pH Ecosystem and the pH Collaborative resident members. The hallmarks of the pH Ecosystem delivery will be collaboration, creativity, collegial working arrangements, data sharing, data driven, resident-centered within a community focus.

The pH Ecosystem Collaborative Council

A pH Ecosystem Collaborative Council composed of representatives from interested members from the various segments within the pH Cooperative will develop, manage and operate the pH Ecosystem Cooperative. This core group will create concepts and design parallel methods to involve citizens in the comprehensive approach to this community-based prevention. Some of the ideas that might emerge are:

The pH Ecosystem Center

The community hospital and/or major medical facility in a community will become a "physical and virtual centerpiece" for healthcare prevention. In the pH Ecosystem the existing community hospital and/or major medical facility evolves into a holistic pH Ecosystem Center. This ecosystem performs the traditional functions of intervention medicine, while, becoming a coordinating center for community-based prevention. Call it a "healthspital," (Dr. Frank Maletz, Surgeon, East Lyme, CT) to recognize and to connote that effective healthcare in local communities needs to connect intervention and prevention into a holistic system with interdependent and connected parts.

In many communities today, the hospital is the largest employer. The delivery mechanisms are fragmented and generally address sickness evaluation, illness diagnosis, disease intervention, and hospitalizations for crisis management, death preparation and intensive care when critical organ systems fail or crash. This has little or nothing to do with wellness, health promotion, or well-being. Each of these foci is directed at keeping the individual alive, not healthy.

Evolving into the pH Ecosystem will require a paradigm shift from sickness and injury to prevention and wellness, an openness to the rest of the community, collaboration with a wide variety of providers and diverse institutions, and the ability to do transformational thinking that leads to transformed services and delivery methods.

The pH Ecosystem Paramedics (Dr.Michael Manning)

The provision of healthcare to individuals will take a radically new approach. No longer will patients travel to locations where services are provided. In the pH Ecosystem, healthcare will come to the pH Cooperative community member as personalized medical and wellness care.

The ultimate goal of a preventive approach to healthcare is for the pH Ecosystem resident member to take the lead role to live healthily. However, the complexity of today's healthcare system complicates the ability for most individuals to take this lead. To enable this transition to personal responsibility for one's health, we envision pH Paramedics as mediators between resident members and traditional healthcare providers. The pH Paramedics will communicate the resident members' understanding of their health to the rest of the healthcare team to assist the pH Paramedics in providing needed medical care at homes of the resident members. Fewer emergency room and hospital visits result in reducing the cost of care and the risk of healthcare acquired illnesses.

As a community-based medical system based on intervention transforms into a pH Ecosystem based on comprehensive preventive healthcare, pH Paramedics will evolve. This new type of practitioner will work alongside doctors, nurse practitioners and physician assistants to deliver patient-centered medical care. They will possess an extensive reach into community life. Today's paramedics have already earned the trust of their neighbors. Often they are the first responders to medical emergencies decisively when minutes and even seconds mean the difference between continuing to enjoy a full life rather than permanent disability or even death. Doctors, nurses, and mid-level providers, like nurse practitioners and physician assistants, will still command respect and be a reservoir of knowledge that will be needed when trauma and acute illness requires specialized care; pH Paramedics will be able to provide personalized wellness and medical treatment at the home and bedside instead of the hospital. Teamed with the local healthspital, they will create a community in which all citizens have the ability to live healthily and at home.

As the focus of healthcare shifts to community-based health promotion and population health, Community Paramedics will make use of the latest developments in information technology:

- pH Paramedics will be trained in the new diagnostic procedures using on-sight sensors, data transfer, and real time suggested treatment through real-time telemedicine links with physicians, nurse practitioners and physician assistants.
- pH Paramedics can monitor patients progress through specialized healthcare apps on the resident members' smart-phones, intervening to changes in a person's healthcare when it becomes an emergency.

An even more exciting role for pH Paramedics will emerge because of their extensive connections with citizens in the communities they serve. Through the training they receive they will be introduced to other aspects of "community transformation" to include weak signal recognition and 21st century creative thinking. They can seed new capacities for transformation in thinking and action through their intimate connections with resident members.

This new role for pH Paramedics will play three key roles as we move to a pH Ecosystem.

Through citizen involvement and home based treatment, pH Paramedics will reduce the cost of healthcare by decreasing costly emergency room visits and hospital stays. This will be accomplished by earlier intervention in chronic disease exacerbations and by shifting the focus of healthcare away from disease treatment to the creation of communities of wellness.

Through a slow increase in the knowledge of future trends in the citizenry, pH Paramedics will improve the economic environment, inspire citizen entrepreneurs, educate new master capacity builders (transformational leaders who have the capacity to help others prepare for a different kind of future), and stimulate the creation of molecular economies at the community level.

The pH Paramedics will provide the potential for new economic opportunities as they interact directly with other pH Ecosystem community members building networks within communities and connecting with other global communities.

The pH Paramedics' emphasis will be on community-based preventive health and wellness care. As in education, the resident members are analogous to students who are becoming the searchers and messengers of content; and the pH Paramedics are like a teacher who is a facilitator of connections and continuous innovation; pH Paramedics will become facilitators and leaders of citizen participation in their own individual healthcare. In this process, they will help create a culture open to new ideas as a result of the collective improvement in knowledge about the emerging future.

Food as Medicine in a pH Ecosystem (Starin McKeen)

Throughout the industrial age the emphasis of food production has been on quantity of macronutrients: producing enough carbohydrates, proteins, and fats to sustain a rapidly growing population throughout increasingly lengthy life-spans. In light of growing health concerns, an abundance of calories, and a pervasive reductionist biomedical model, micronutrient supplementation has gained popularity with little effect on the health status of the global population. The food system of the future will undergo a significant restructuring to allow for a systemic approach to breeding, cultivation, distribution, and storage to *enhance* phytonutrient and antioxidant content and concentration in foods with potent preventive health properties.

Phytonutrients, commonly referred under umbrella terms as antioxidants or bioactive molecules, fluctuate throughout the plant lifecycle in response to climate, environmental stress, pests, and pathogens, via genetic and epigenetic regulation. Phytonutrients also act as defense molecules in humans, fighting holistically against inflammation and oxidative free radicals, while promoting healthy enzyme activity and a robust gut flora. Currently documented actions include anti-carcinogenic, anti-tumorigenic, anti-inflammation, anti-plaque, anti-obesogenic, glucose-stabilization, pre- and pro-biotic, and increased metabolic activity. Humans evolved with plants and their respective phytonutrients; we will be highly dependent on them in the fight to reduce and prevent chronic disease and increasing climate and environmental stresses.

Phytonutrients are typically bitter and pungent, which has contributed to the systematic removal of these health-promoting molecules from our current market-oriented food system via selective breeding and removal of environmental stresses (e.g. pesticides). This action has both decreased concentration in individual varieties, and drastically narrowed the diversity of phytonutrient molecules present throughout the food system. Long distance distribution is the other greatest phytonutrient offender, requiring fruits to be picked before maturity, and facilitating rapid degradation during transport between harvest and consumption.

As awareness and understanding of phytonutrient activity increases, healthcare professionals will begin taking an active role with plant breeders and producers to insure patients can include phytonutrient dense cultivars in daily diets. The approach to get these varieties onto plates will be incredibly multifaceted, demanding a highly localized, highly integrated distribution system. Year-round, climate-resilient, hyper-local produce production must be the norm. A priority of this production will be to incorporate diverse varieties: cultivars will be pulled out of germ plasm banks and made widely available to the public. Requests from doctors, patients, restaurant managers, students, and everyday consumers will dictate the open-source breeding programs, and provide direct guidance on preferences for flavor, novelty, and health.

Micro-greenhouses, employing high efficiency, low-water technology will speckle cities, most notably at schools, hospitals, high density housing complexes, outside business cafeterias, and franchised casual restaurants. Students will harvest their own produce for lunch, while learning about plant life cycles, complex sustainable systems, preventive nutrition, and greater edible biodiversity. Their knowledge will transfer upwards to heads of households, supported by doctor's dietary recommendations and referrals, and significantly increased accessibility both at home and away. This abundance of plant-based foods will contribute to drastically decreased food waste, by removing the waste incurred through transport and distribution, and funneling excess back into composting systems that support both plant and fish production.

Larger urban research farms will support the dispersed micro-greenhouses by raising plants to near-maturity and producing larger varieties using sustainable techniques such as aquaponics, natural pollinators, and ecosystem-based pest management. These research farms will be the powerhouses that synthesize increasingly large data into consumer-friendly terms. High throughput analysis and exponentially increasing data capacity will allow for big plant data to be integrated with big market and nutrition data, creating a new paradigm for transparency that facilitates preventive health, biodiversity enhancement, and sustainable production of our most valuable and perishable edible resources.

As the pH Ecosystem Cooperative focuses upon preventive health, it can share among its members the evolving information on food, its production, and its preventive characteristics. It can also provide a laboratory to test the efficacy of both production and preventive qualities.

By now the reader may have noticed that the use of inter-locking networks and ecosystems is fundamental to the creation of "comprehensive community transformation." This is a challenge to local areas, especially smaller communities, whose leaders are usually limited to traditional thinking, limited in money available and used to command and control types of leadership.

It is our premise that in a time of interconnectedness and exponential change, that deeply collaborative networks will be necessary to react quickly with enough knowledge and resources to be able to deal with such complex issues such as climate change, an interdependent global economy and comprehensive medicine and community-based systems of preventive healthcare. There will be a need for expanded numbers of Transformational Leaders who are Master Capacity Builders to be able to have the capacity to see connections among different networks, know how to spot weak signals and understand their potential impact and seed transformational ways of thinking and action in local communities.

Building pH Ecosystem Connections to Other Key Community Capacities

Pools of healthcare, community and neighborhood leaders can be introduced to the concept of a pH Ecosystem Holarchy. Simultaneously, they can be introduced to the new concept of Transformational Leadership to develop new skills to "build capacities for transformation." Building these "parallel processes" requires three actions. Assuring an understanding of how this systemic concept is organized and how various elements will be key to a community-based approach to wellness. Building "interlocking networks" of interested healthcare professionals, community leaders, and citizens involved with systemic pilot efforts that can be scaled up. Designing current projects and research and development processes to help citizens and leaders understand the "aha!" stage of community transformation.

A key to the success of all phases and stages of an emerging community pH Ecosystem will be inspiring a sufficient number of Master Capacity Builders able to seed and facilitate the emergent sub-systems of the overall Holarchy.

The pH Ecosystem and Economic Development (Jim Damicis)

We are living in a time of economic and social transformation. For the last ten years and for the next fifteen years, there has been and will be an ongoing transition from an Industrial Economy to what some futurists call a Creative Molecular Economy (CME). It is defined as:

An economy based on the integration of emerging radical technologies, with creative individuals, small groups and companies organized in interlocking networks, connecting and disconnecting constantly in processes of continuous innovation.

In biology, the body is a complex system. As previously stated, community-based healthcare is also a CAS (complex adaptive system) with many interrelated parts influencing care and outcomes. For economic development, local and regional economies are CAS and thus warrant an understanding of the interrelated components, influences, and networks that make them up. This can be used to help create community based preventive health care systems focused on wellness that are important to the health of local and regional economies.

The healthcare system is an important part of a significant majority of local and regional economies contributing significantly to the number of businesses and levels of employment and wages.

In 2013, employment in the healthcare and social assistance sector totaled nearly 14.5 million jobs representing 12% of all jobs in the U.S. These jobs were contained within 1.2 million establishments. This was the highest level of all the major employment sectors.

Between 2004 and 2013, the healthcare and social assistance sector added 3.3 million jobs, the most among all sectors in terms of job growth. This represented a growth rate of 22% over the ten-year period. And growth is projected to continue. Between 2013 and 2022 the healthcare and social assistance sector is projected to add another 3.8 million jobs (most among all major sectors), an increase of 21%.

Also in 2013 there were another 3.9 million jobs in industry sectors closely related to healthcare including Pharmaceutical and Medicine Manufacturing, Medical Equipment and Supplies Manufacturers and wholesalers, pharmacies and healthcare stores, testing laboratories, Research and Development entities, and state and local government hospitals.

The impact of healthcare on local and regional economies goes well beyond businesses, jobs, wages and direct economic inputs and outputs. The level of access to and quality of healthcare determines individual wellness and, in turn, the well-being of communities and regions. Community wellness impacts productivity and increased quality of life to support worker and resident happiness. Community wellness is a major component to attract entrepreneurs and grow companies.

Even with all of these significant impacts and potential benefits, the healthcare sector is often not a focus for economic developers. There are several reasons for this. First, it is often seen as "out of one's" control because of healthcare bureaucracy (laws, regulations, insurance, etc.). Economic developers feel there is little they can do to influence decision making within the context of economic development. Second, is not viewed as an export-intensive industry bringing in wealth from outside the local and regional boundaries. Third, except for the top science and tech-intensive specialty occupations such as doctors, many of the jobs including medical technicians and support typically pay low to moderate wages. Fourth, the industry outlook is often distorted by the financial and bureaucratic challenges of the larger institutions within the industry, primarily hospitals, causing emerging opportunities in new, innovative, small, and niche markets and businesses to be overlooked. Lastly, when healthcare is considered, it is not typically seen as part of a complex, comprehensive community/regional system that cuts across all economic and social sectors with diverse stakeholders.

Because of the significant impacts on economic, community, and individual health, the healthcare sector will become a focus of economic development efforts at the local and regional level. Since it is a CAS operating within local and regional economies that are also becoming increasing dynamic and complex, the principles and tools of the Creative Molecular Economy offer a pathway for successful economic development planning, implementing, and adaption.

The Creative Molecular Economy stresses the importance of self-organizing, interlocking networks as the primary method for organizing, planning, and decision making. In healthcare, there is a diverse set of individual and organizations that impact individual and community health and economic outcomes. These include:

- Healthcare service providers – hospitals, nursing homes, home health providers, pharmacies, and specialists in alternative medicines.
- Social services providers.
- Insurance providers.
- Nutrition and food providers/producers.
- Recreation service providers.
- Local and regional government – in particular public health, public safety.
- Education – all levels both as involved in education and training but also health, nutrition, and recreation provision.
- Entrepreneurs and small businesses.
- Economic, community, and workforce developers.

All of these should be part of the development and implementation of a comprehensive community-based, preventive healthcare system of wellness that is integrated with economic development.

The future of healthcare will include community-based prevention and wellness research and development as well as traditional intervention built around emerging best practices. There will be constant change and little, if anything, will be standard in the future. Consequently, leaders in the healthcare arena as well as community leaders will need to become familiar with the theory and practical application of complex adaptive systems.

The World Economic Forum's Future Risks Reports of 2012 and 2013 emphasized the need for a "reconceptualization of society's institutions," as well as the need to create "capacities for resiliency," if the communities of our nations were to become vital and sustainable in an emerging era of constant change. Nowhere will these ideas be more important than in the future of healthcare. Not surprisingly, the principles and practical application of complex adaptive systems will be at the center of the toolbox of community transformation. These transformational ideas and skills will be used by leaders who recognize the need to shift from traditional healthcare based on intervention, to a holarchy of ideas and methods that connect community-based prevention with intervention, a Ph Ecosystem Holarchy.

A 'pH Ecosystem' Futures Project

Sample Strategy Proposal Worksheet

Seeding Community Transformation

Emerging Idea, Weak Signal, Discovery	Potential Impact
Health: Develop "Home Based" Healthcare	A shift to the concept of "home-based healthcare" will be a key part of a community-based approach to prevention as a focus on healthcare compared to the present focus of intervention.

Strategy For Building Capacities:

1. Create a team of medical professionals, technologists and non-profits to design and implement a "medical home" project.
2. Recruit IBM or other technology firms to be involved as cosponsors.
3. Establish multiple networks of citizens who have varying health needs to be a part of the project.
4. Involve the "smart toilet" concept as a part of digital medical monitoring.
5. Establish an evaluation system that will provide an evidence of improved healthcare at a lower cost.

Expected Outcomes:

1   Families become committed to good nutrition and a routine of exercise.

2   Develop treatment methodologies that are personalized.

3   Simplify how healthcare is delivered.

4   Create incentives that reward treatment based on evidence-based outcomes.

5   Utilize the technologies of a "digital home" to organize and analyze personalized healthcare data.

Conclusion

This systemic approach for preparing a community for a different kind of healthcare is consistent with the other chapters in this book. In all cases, the idea of identifying emerging weak signals to create a futures context is key. To be able to build capacities for transformation, a new approach to leadership is needed. With this in mind, we have introduced the idea of Transformational Leadership and Master Capacity Builders. Our Industrial Economy is presently morphing through a transition Knowledge Economy to a very entrepreneurial Creative Molecular Economy. We have posited that our present system of democracy has reached its limits of usefulness and that Polycentric Democracy and Mobile Collaborative Governance is in the process of evolving. For our economic and governance systems to remain vital and sustainable in a time of great, transformational change, we have introduced the idea that our institutions, especially our educational ideas and methods, need to be reconceptualized, with capacities for transformation developed in all areas of community life through futures research and development processes and projects.

All of these newly emerging ideas will need to be developed in parallel processes, emerging in different ways and at different rates. This new approach to planning for the future is called adaptive planning, and will require design teams of Master Capacity Builders to come together and create innovative ideas and methods as a system of "comprehensive community transformation."

We started this book with a chapter on the need for a new philosophical framework that we call the "Second Enlightenment." We end this book in the same way with the admonition that too many leaders and citizens want quick answers with little struggle necessary. This will not happen. We live in a time of historical transformation that is chaotic and, at times, seems out of control.

That is because we live in a time that is out of control in the sense that new undergirding principles are emerging as we move from the norms of independence, hyper competition, radical individuality and linear thinking and action, to a time that will be based on interdependence, deep collaboration, connected individuality and non-linear, systemic thinking and action.

The world is out of control not only in terms of speed and irrationality, but even more important, out of control in terms of lack of predictability, ambiguity and uncertainty. It makes great sense that we cannot use the principles, concepts, methods and techniques of an Industrial Age. We need a new philosophic approach based on a Second Enlightenment, an Ecological Civilization, Transformational Learning and Leadership, Polycentric Democracy and Creative Molecular Economy.

The ideas in this book don't provide a traditional road map because a road map is based on a specific set of directions that is already known and defined. What this book offers is a framework of new concepts and methods to provide a new way of looking at the future, a set of ideas, concepts and methods that may help you connect dots that have been floating around in your head.

We are all being carried along in the "Rapids of Change" about which our old friend and colleague, Robert Theobald, wrote two decades ago. If we have been able to help you get to the "hmm?" stage of transformation, and even a few "ahas!" we have succeeded with our book.

Although the future seems more challenging that ever, we need to remember that our forefathers faced similar historical transformation without the knowledge and tools of today. What we need to recapture is their spirit of adventure and their commitment to making the world a better place, whatever risk and fears they experienced. Now is not a time to look for the safety of emotional cocoons. Now is the time for exploring a new kind of future, arm and arm with each other to create, seed and evolve radical ideas as a result of this time of historical transformation.

Epilogue

Now what? What is your notion of time and of the future regarding deep change? All of the things we have talked about in this book and in many of the things we do or are responsible for in our daily lives are framed by some expectation upon how soon something will be enacted.

From the rise of the Second Enlightenment to the evolution of Transformational Learning, electronically engaged governance, the emerging Creative Molecular Economy and a new community-based approach to preventive healthcare, all these emerging ideas and movements will require significant collaboration, effort and time, and require a call to action by those who believe that the world we hand off to our grandchildren can be better than the one in which we currently live.

In the epochs of society and life of a community there are constantly evolving, repeating rhythms around multiple calendars including government and the terms of elected officials, the school calendar, and multiple budget cycles for many municipal agencies. There are family calendars including holidays and activities and many more. All of these things influence our notion of time and how fast transformative change can happen. Most often, many people feel there is not enough time to accomplish all the things we would like to undertake.

Creating transformational communities within the context of an emerging future quite different from the past will require helping people see that transformational change is possible while recognizing how great a challenge it is when there is no template by which to go. The emerging ideas in this book such as 21st Century Neighborhood Academies or Future Forward Colleges or the pH Ecosystem for preventive healthcare, reflect practical efforts of research and development by many collaborators over twenty-six years … and due to the immensity of the historical challenge, we are just beginning. The timing is right. We urge you to join our COTF International Network of self-organizing individuals who are committed to pursue research and development for comprehensive community transformation. Using the frameworks in this book to help frame new approaches whether creating more effective community colleges or a better way to govern, we recommend the important virtue of patience.

Leaders and change practitioners who are seeking immediate gratification are setting themselves up for disappointment. The community you are looking to transform itself will need time to learn new principles, methods and techniques for community transformation. In all cases, communities and people change in increasingly complex ways. We recommend that you start in small non-linear ways using the concept of parallel processes. A Master Capacity Builder who is particularly adept at using the tools in this book knows that as we move through stages of change we can accelerate transformation but we cannot skip steps if we want quality and long lasting impact.

In our experience, we have seen the following patterns emerge in the development and response to a community or organizational challenge.

Communities are just like any other living system and go through predictable overarching stages (however, the details are unique) in responding to a threat or a crisis.

Seven Principles of Transformational Change

- Identify Emerging Crises: Crisis or challenge emerges in community or organization and begins to unfold in time.

- Identify Weak Signals: Challenges appear and mutate into complex issues that only a few people begin to sense.

- Utilize Crisis to seed capacities for transformation: In this stage sequence the crisis is perceived as a threat by the larger community or organization.

- Dissonance: Most challenges particularly ones germinating from public institutions have developed over a period of time. At first, there is confusion about how to respond to a crisis and no sense of how to move forward.

- Core group convenes: In response to crisis a core group is formed by leaders to acknowledge and address crisis. It is in this stage; Master Capacity Builder skills are first utilized. There is often a tension between folks who are advocating for a traditional response and with those seeking to affect transformational change. We advocate for parallel processes in which short-term traditional responses are coupled with adaptive or transformational processes.

- Resurgence: As the core group responds to the evolving crisis, there will be small signs of progress or success with "low hanging fruit" objectives in the short term. In the short term, using traditional and adaptive planning and response processes in parallel will insure that seeds of future success are planted as different "access points" are identified. Always remember that for community transformation to occur, a system of parallel processes is needed for different reasons ... yet, always to help other build capacities for transformation.

- Dynamic Equilibrium: As more capacities for transformation take root, a sense of ownership will emerge within the community, and a tipping point of community transformation will begin to emerge.

Throughout American history significant change has taken time to occur. People need to come to a personal judgment or decision point that change is necessary and worth their sacrifice of commitment, time and effort. Our experience shows that transformational change takes much longer than expected for a critical mass of citizens to agree how to deal with current issues and emerging complexity when there is no road map by which to go and processes of traditional strategic planning increasingly ineffective. Seeding transformational ideas about how to prepare for the future will challenge the belief system of most people, especially key ideas of how they see the world. Whereas you will experience resistance or bewilderment from many folks, remember that at the core of resistance to change is usually some ingrained fear. Each of us can represent the best of what the century has bequeathed us. If you find one key idea in this book that connects with you, our time has been well spent. We ask that you get involved with the idea of community transformation by talking to one person about any idea that has been shared. We would love to hear from you about your ideas of transformation, and, as our good friend, Dr. Frank Maletz always says, we leave you with his call to action: "Look forward, always forward!"

The Language of Community Transformation

There is a reason for leaders to learn a new language to help prepare their local areas for the future. It is very simple. Old words and old phrases that are readily understood explain a time gone by and were developed for an Industrial Society based on hierarchies, standard rules and linear thinking. In this time of historical transformation, our society is morphing into a structure of networks, webs and non-linear dynamics. The old language does not fit the new realities as our society grows more complex and interactive, connecting and disconnecting peoples, organizations and ideas at will. The coming age requires leaders who understand the need to "uplearn" and function at a higher level of complexity and competence. The following introduces words and phrases important to the leadership role for community transformation in communities.

Access Point: That opening of any system or situation which allows an opportunity to introduce a new idea, method or connection.

And/Both Thinking: The capacity to see direct, indirect or oblique connections in everything without having to identify one best answer.

Biological Principles: Establishing initial conditions, designing parallel processes, interdependence and system thinking, connecting disparate ideas and processes, emergence of ideas and outcomes from dialogue, feedback based on what occurs, self-organization and adapting to changing conditions.

Capacities for Transformation: New abilities, skills and

knowledge that support individual, organizational and community transformation that redefines the in-kind nature and scope of each entity.

Community Transformation: Community Transformation is the concept of preparing local communities for a constantly changing, interdependent and increasingly complex society by challenging traditional assumptions of we educate/learn, how we do economic development, how we lead, how we govern, even how we think.

Complex Adaptive Systems: The design and interaction of living systems that change and adapt according to changes in the environment.

Creative Molecular Economy: A new type of economy that is emerging from the last stages of an industrial economy based on manufacturing to an organic economy based on creativity, biological principles that will be self- organizing and genetic engineering methods that will produce products. Advanced cloud computing will be a key technology to support the new type of economy.

Direct Consensus Democracy: A parallel approach to local decision making that is based on citizen control and ownership of each of three stages:

1. Identify key issues
2. Define key factors to understand most important issue/s identified
3. Develop alternative strategies for citizens to choose.

Electronic Infrastructure: The interconnection of computers, sensors and wireless technology which forms a comprehensive network of digital sharing of data, information and knowledge.

Futures Context: A framework of ideas, trands and weak signals that emphasize a total shift of environment and thinking into new paradigms that are emerging.

Futures Generative Dialogue: The ability to collaborate and develop innovations through dialogue within a futures context.

Interdependence: The capacity of multiple factors, people and organizations to interact and help each other succeed.

Master Capacity Builder: The type of leader who understands the need to help citizens in local communities learn to think within a futures context and is able to build "capacities for transformation" in each other, one's organization and in local areas. A traditional leader focuses on the short term. A Master Capacity Builder focuses on the short and long term.

Molecular Economy: The smallest unit that is the basis for organizing a Creative Molecular Economy or community transformation process, whether individuals, or small groups and networks.

Mutual Collaborative Coaching: The process of a network or team of facilitating, transformational leaders who learn from each other as they collaborate to design and develop "comprehensive community transformation".

Organic: What things we make and how we make them will tied to understanding and reading life and to programming life for specific purposes. Processes are considered organic if initial conditions are set, and emergence occurs as a result of the interaction of people, ideas or networks...without premeditated outcomes expected.

Parallel Processes: The new method of using complementary processes to focus on different needs of any changing complex adaptive system. One example is to use strategic planning for short term community development needs at the same time that adaptive planning is used to develop and nurture new capacities for the future.

Transformative Leadership: A new type of leadership that emphasizes new ways of thinking and relationship building in order to develop capacities for transformation for the longer run in parallel to short term oriented traditional, outcomes based leadership. Both are needed.

Transformational Learning; The concept of learning that integrates the need to expand knowledge, (to include trends and weak signals) ask appropriate questions within a futures context and connect diverse and disparate ideas for purpose of continuous innovation.

Transformational Thinking: There are three capacities of trans-formational thinking:

1 Ability to think at different levels, for different reasons, at different times
2 Ability to connect disparate ideas
3 Ability to identify emerging weak signals and new knowledge as a part of a creative process.

Uplearning: The ability to think and understand at a more complex level.

Weak Signals: Emerging new ideas, inventions, innovations and discoveries that are not yet trends, but have the potential to make an impact on society.

Webs and Networks: The building blocks of a community transformation as a result of moving faster, in interconnected ways and to a higher level of complexity.

21st Century Bibliography

Barabasi, A (2002) Linked: The New Science of Networks, Cambridge, MA: Perseus Books

Benyus, J (1997) Biomimicry, New York, NY: William Morrow

Bohm, D (1989) On Dialogue, Ojai, CA: Self Published

Brynjolfsson, E & McAffee A (2014), The Second Machine Age, New York, NY: Norton

Berman, M (2000) The Dark Ages of America, New York, NY: Norton

Canton, J (2006) The Extreme Future, New York, Penguin Books

Carey, K (2015) The End of College, New York, NY: Riverhead Books

Diamandis , P & Kotler, S (2015) Bold, New York, NY: Simon & Schuster

Enriquez, J (2001) As the Future Catches You, New York, NY: Three Rivers Press

Farley, J & Daly, H (2004) Ecological Economics, Washington, DC: Island Press

Gilding, P (2011) The Great Disruption, New York, NY: Bloomsbury Press

Hwang, V & Horowitt, G (2012) The Rainforest, Los Altos, CA: Regenwald

Isaacs, W (2008), Dialogue: The Art of Thinking Together, New York, NY: Doubleday

Jacoby, S (2008) The Age of American Unreason, New York, NY: Vintage Books

Johnson, S (2001) Emergence, New York, NY: Scribner

Koestler, A (1967) The Ghost in the Machine, New York, NY: Macmillan

Kaipa, P & Radjou, N (2013) From Smart to Wise, San Francisco, CA: Jossey-Bass

Kunstler, J (2005) The Long Emergency, New York, NY: Grove

Press

Lederman, L & Hill, C (2011) Quantum Physics for Poets, Amherst, NY: Prometheus Books

Liu, E & Hanaur, N (2011) The Gardens of Democracy, Seattle, WA: Sasquatch Books

Lipton, B & Bhaerman, S (2009) Spontaneous Evolution, New York, NY: Hay House

Meyer, C & Davis, S (2003) It's Alive, New York, NY: Crown Business Books

Nichtern, E (2007) One City, Somerset, MA: Wisdom Publications

Pink, D (2005) A Whole New Mind, New York, NY: Riverhead Books

Ogle, R (2007) Smart World, Cambridge, MA: Harvard Business School Press

Postrel, V (1998) The Future and Its Enemies, New York, NY: Free Press

Ramo, J.C. (2007) The Age of the Unthinkable, New York, NY: Back Bay Books

Ricards, J (2011) The Currency Wars, New York, NY: Penguin Books

Rifkin, J (2011) The Third Industrial Revolution, Basingstoke, United Kingdom: Palgrave Macmillan

Ross, C (2011) The Leaderless Revolution, New York, NY: Penguin Books

Strauss, B & Howe, N (1997) The Fourth Turning, New York, NY: Broadway Books

Taleb, N (2007) Black Swan, New York, NY: Random House

Tapscott, D (2009) Grown Up Digital, New York, NY: McGraw Hill

Thomson, C (2014) Full Spectrum Intelligence, Alresford, Hants, United Kingdom

Toffler, A (1980) The Third Wave, New York, NY: Bantam Books

Tuomi, I (2002) Networks of Innovation, Oxford, United Kingdom: Oxford University Press

Venter, C (2013) Life at the Speed of Light, New York, NY: Penguin Books

Wilber, K (2006) A Brief History of Everything, Boston, MA: Shambhala Publications

About the Authors

Rick Smyre is an internationally recognized futurist specializing in the area he helped originate called "community transformation." A graduate of Davidson College and NC State University, Mr. Smyre has four degrees and is President of the Center for Communities of the Future. Increasingly known for his work as an author of the concept of a Second Enlightenment, he is also an architect of the new field of "molecular leadership." Mr. Smyre served on the staff of the National Economic Development Institute for fourteen years.

Married for 52 years to Brownie Allen, Mr. Smyre has three children, Cinda (50), Deric (48), and Beth (45). In the '70s he was the CEO of a textile yarn spinning firm. As a result of his experience at the local, state and national levels, he understands issues local communities face when preparing for a different kind of economy and society.

Mr. Smyre's work emphasizes innovative concepts, methods, and techniques connected with the Communities of the Future idea in collaboration with a network of over 1000 individuals in forty-seven states and thirteen countries. The focus of this work is to develop "capacities for transformation" in the thinking and activities of citizen leaders in local communities, His articles have been published on various websites, and three essays, *Beyond the Deck Chairs, It Is More Than Either/Or,* and *The Three Triangles of Transformation* by the World Future Society in 1998, 2004 and 2007. 'Preparing 21st Century Rural Economies' is a chapter in *Knowledge-Based Economy,* published in India in 2006. Two articles on his vision of higher education were published in June 2008 in the book, *Careers in Bioengineering and Biotechnology.* His recent article, *Searching for a Second Enlightenment* was published as a chapter in the book, *For Our Commin Home* in 2015. Mr. Smyre has coauthored numerous articles published on the web journals of Johns Hopkins University, The World Future Society and the

American Association of Community College Trustees.

Mr. Smyre focuses his work in several ways. He speaks internationally and has provided over 400 seminars, keynotes and retreats over the last decade. Of special interest to Mr. Smyre is his work to help local communities prepare for transformational change: 1) as a strategic networker to develop and apply new ideas such as the Second Enlightenment, Transformation Learning and a Creative Molecular Economy, and 2) as a "master capacity builder" to work with local community leaders to help them develop 21st century transformational leadership skills for community transformation.

rlsmyre@aol.com

Neil Richardson is a strategist and a public servant who specializes in smart government advocacy and integral thinking. Neil has degrees from the University of South Florida and Georgetown University. He has worked on civil society building in Ghana and across the United States including organizing large-scale voter observation initiatives, civic engagement and strategic planning processes. He has served as a policy adviser for three Mayors in the District of Columbia. Neil currently serves as Director of Advancement, Partnerships and Continuing Education at the University of the District of Columbia where he is a founding member of the team that launched the District's first community college. Rick and Neil have been collaborating for more than 15 years as part of the Communities of the Future network. Neil founded Integral Action, a strategy firm to work with thought leaders and next generation elected officials on ways to engage the public with authenticity and foresight. Neil is also the founder of www.waltwhitmanmeditation.com that advocates for a unique secular meditation that is based on his original research about Whitman's practice that led to his transcendent insight and poetry.

neilrichardsondc@gmail.com

Let's stay connected!

Please stay connected to Rick and Neil by visiting the
Communities of the Future website:

http://www.communitiesofthefuture.org
www.communitiesofthefuture.org

We will posting the latest the ideas, trends and weak signals
from across our international network. Together we can take a
step forward in creating a world where people can thrive in
communities that honor all parts of civilization and the planet.

Never doubt that a small group of thoughtful, committed citizens can change the world, It is the only thing that ever has.
Margaret Meade

A Resource for Master Capacity Builders

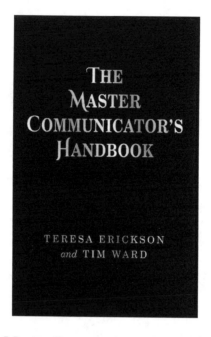

The Master Communicator's Handbook
by Teresa Erickson and Tim Ward

This book is for people who want to change the world. To put the ideas of *Preparing for a World that Doesn't Exist - Yet* into practice and build Communities of the Future, you need to communicate. You need to know how to collaborate, facilitate, co-create, and to seed new ideas. In these pages, Ward and Erickson share with you what they learned over 30 years as professional communicators and advisors to leaders of global organizations. Their goal is to give future Master Capacity Builders the communications tools they need to be effective catalysts for transformation.

ISBN 978-1-78535-153-2
bulk orders: Contact Changemakers
Books, mary@jhpbooks.net

CHANGE
MAKERS
BOOKS

Changemakers publishes books for individuals committed to transforming their lives and transforming the world. Our readers seek to become positive, powerful agents of change. Changemakers books inform, inspire, and provide practical wisdom and skills to empower us to create the next chapter of humanity's future.

Please visit our website at www.changemakers-books.com